The SoftSpot

Published in 2023 by OurSoftSpot.com
675 Biltmore Avenue – Suite G
Asheville, North Carolina, 28803
United States of America
(828) 252-8390

Cover, Layout and Art Work: Pieter Van Tonder

ISBN: 978-1-7349273-1-3

Psychology

Copyright: 2023 – Carl Mumpower, Ph.D.
All rights reserved.

Reproduction and translation of any part of this work beyond that permitted by Sections 107 and 108 of the United States Copyright Act without the permission of the copyright owner is unlawful.

For more information— www.drmumpower.com

- Dedication -

This book is dedicated to my wife – Lisa – and my able assistant – Pam. Their shared quiet positive touch has been a matchless source of support, magnification, and energy.

Both mirror a majority of people who face life with a steady dedication to doing good things without fuss or fanfare.

It is through such people that our world retains its balance.

Admiration is rarely generous for the parents, officers of the law, hands-on doers, soldiers, teachers, healthcare providers, ministers, principle driven politicians, and others who live lives of quiet invisibility while doing the right thing for the right reasons.

In a world seemingly overwhelmed with the struggling, people – like Lisa and Pam – are truly the best of us.

With gratitude,

Carl Mumpower – July 4th, 2023

Praise for The SoftSpot

"A tremendously helpful book. Nothing is sugar coated…an insightful guide to tackling life's challenges with meaningful, dedicated action." — K

"It was easy for me to get lost in my thoughts and become irritated with myself. Reading The SoftSpot helped me understand why and how to stop being so hard on me." — A

"Dr. M gives an insightful, encouraging take on the ways we lose and recover ourselves. He challenges and uplifts with deep words of wisdom." — D

"Until I read this book, I had no understanding of my never-ending cycle of draining myself and recovering myself and draining myself again. Now I get it and I know how to change it." — S

"I don't like to read, and so I liked the format of The SoftSpot. I didn't have to endure pages of boring stuff to get to the good stuff. That helped me absorb this wonderful book's really good stuff." — W

"After reading this author's previous book The One Percenter, I was drawn by the title of this new one. There is truth and grace here that offers a bright and clear path to a whole new world." — P

"I feel so blessed by the information I've learned from The Softspot. It has taught me new ways to maintain my goodness and hope in the face of challenging darkness. I cannot recommend this book more highly." — A

- Content -

Chapter One - Something to Know 1

Chapter Two - The Gift 9

Chapter Three - Life is Not Easy 21

Chapter Four - Soft Spots 34

Chapter Five - The Theft 54

Chapter Six - Taking Care 66

Chapter Seven - Replenishment 78

Chapter Eight - A Simple Script 87

Chapter Nine - Hard Spots 105

Chapter Ten - It Takes a Team 121

Chapter Eleven - Soft Wisdom 161

Chapter Twelve - Assembly 188

Chapter Thirteen - Leftovers 199

Chapter Fourteen - Hard or Soft 221

Chapter Fifteen - Softspot Wisdoms 228

Chapter Sixteen - In the End 238

In Closing 250

Consider the firefly — the darker the night,
the brighter it's light...

- Introduction -

"Softspots" – that term first came to mind some twenty-five years ago as a framework for explaining the unexplainable.

Through my years of training and practice, I continually ran into things that traditional psychology, spirituality, and worldly scientific insights could not explain.

Along the way I became determined to find a way to better understand and define these mysteries.

I kept notes and vowed to myself that I would not write the book until I personally understood and could do the things I was writing about.

Over time and many hurdles, I reached that point, and thereby earned permission to translate what I have learned.

What follows is less an attempt to demonstrate academic insights than to embrace practical ones. There are things shared here that will fluster the scholar as surely as they will delight the truth-seeker.

This book was a team effort. Every person I have seen through the many years of practice – literally thousands – has taught me as surely as I have worked to teach them.

Thus comes The SoftSpot. Two hundred and fifty plus pages of what I have come to understand about the complexities, challenges, and nuances of building a good life on a hard world. There is great hope in knowing it can be done.

I am grateful for the opportunity to explain the way to how.

Chapter One

Something to Know

You were born into a world with things, like sand, that are in seemingly endless supply. Other things, like diamonds, are precious and rare.

You are told about these things.

Inside you are things that are even more priceless and unique than diamonds. They hold potency and power beyond measure and, similarly, their supply is distinctly limited.

You are not told about these things.

- Necessary Things -

There once was a tiny droplet of joy. It brimmed with energy, hope, and love. It delighted in the gift of life. Goodness, gratitude, and greatness were its birthright – all directed to the deepest potentials of its host.

With the right pinch of nurture, the spot grew effortlessly. The bloom of health was its evident legacy, and setbacks were but brief challenges dependably ending in progress.

But something changed. Amidst the temptations of a hardened world, the host began to live carelessly, impatiently, dishonestly. His drive became singular – to feel what was pleasant, escape what was not, and avoid the costs. Thought and action became captives to this passion.

As ever-darker decisions were made toward an unquenchable thirst, the little spot began to struggle. Vitality and joy were replaced by fatigue and despair. Surrounding spots retreated, shrank, and disappeared, never to return.

The end was painless. It simply ceased to be. With its death, a little bit of light went out in the human. For that tiny spot bore a great charge – the essence of life itself.

Now that 'they' were gone, so too was his vigor, courage, compassion, and so many other necessary things. As with all bad ends, denial was there to mask his discomfort.

The host did not understand the impact of his careless ways, but he did feel his growing emptiness. Sometimes he imagined that the core of his being had been flushed away.

He was right…

We are born into a complex and demanding world.

Blessings and breaks come mixed with trials and dangers.

Those forces that seek to harm us are varied and many.

They hide amidst that which is pleasant and good.

Sometimes they even pretend to be good.

But there is a difference in that which *feels* good and *is* good.

"The demon is a liar. He will lie to confuse us; but he will also mix lies with the truth to attack us. His attack is psychological, Damien. And powerful." — William Peter Blatty, The Exorcist

Life is filled with confusions.

It can be hard to separate the good from the bad.

We are all vulnerable in this search.

But we are not powerless.

To help with our journey, we are each given a bucket.

Just one.

"Do not free a camel of the burden of his hump; you may be freeing him from being a camel." — G.K. Chesterton

Some of our buckets are small and some are large.

They come in many colors, styles, and textures.

Like snowflakes, every single one is different.

And it is what is held inside that makes them special.

Hidden in our buckets are gems of boundless potential.

They are, in fact, the lifeblood of our existence.

"Even the invisible leave footprints." — Wayne Gerard Trotman

In the newness of life, our buckets come filled to the brim...

...with spots of cheer, peace, warmth, and other good things.

These are our *soft spots*.

And they are mysterious and precious.

They grow in the light, but starve in the dark.

They are both strong and fragile.

And they are irreplaceably essential to *everything* we are.

"The cause is hidden. The effect is visible to all." — Ovid

That importance is rarely valued in our self-important world.

Our planet's inhabitants reliably seek their own gratification.

In that selfish search, there is a tendency to confuse:

>*Conformity* with *cooperation*.
>*Childishness* with *cleverness*.
>*Carelessness* with *courage*.
>*Control* with *conviction*.
>*Corrupting* with *caring*.
>*Chatter* with *character*.

Soft spots are designed to help us navigate these confusions.

Without them, we become like a cloud without rain.

"The danger is that of coming to love the prison." — C.S. Lewis

Soft spots come with five very important considerations.

1. They are breakable.

2. Repairing them is hard.

3. They are limited in number.

4. They are each made just for us.

5. Once they are gone, they are mostly gone.

"But no one seems to know that we need to know these things. One shouldn't gamble with what is irreplaceable and precious."
— Naomi Klein

Chapter Two

The Gift

Life is a present. It comes packaged with special things that serve as your life spark. These things function as an irreplaceable bridge to all that is good in the human experience, both on earth and beyond.

We are all born with constraints on the number of these things. That number cannot be sidestepped, shirked, or switched. When they die from abuse or neglect, they leave a void that is rarely refilled.

Not all that is good or bad in life can be seen, heard, or otherwise sensed. There are some things that resist the exploitable temptations of science, the arts, religion, and enterprise.

These unknowns are a bedrock of a self-correcting world. Without their restraining influence, appetites for control, pleasure, and other seductions would destroy us all.

- There are No Shortcuts -

Growing up was a study in chaos.

It was a constant struggle between feast and famine, joy and fear, normal and crazy. Figuring out one's place in that mess felt like writing in a diary while jumping rope. It couldn't be done.

There were nice moments, but life didn't really begin until he graduated at seventeen and stumbled upon a quote about it being important for a man "participate in the events of his time and people." That meant a trip to Vietnam. His time there created a wobbly bridge to an interest in psychology.

Looking back now, he can see that in the seventies, we knew and did more to help people with mental health problems than we do now. The evolution of symptom-relieving medication and bureaucracy-driven go-through-the-motions treatment have proven their limitations.

There are reasons for this regression. Along the way his profession began embracing the pretense that it was possible to live irresponsibly and feel good at the same time. We can see the folly of this deception all around us in twenty-first century America.

Forty-five years of practice in psychology has affirmed one stark truth: there are no pills, practices, promises, or pretensions that can enable us to side-step our individual accountability for the care and feeding of our gifts.

Understanding this uncheatable reality is an irreplaceable foundation for health in all its forms...

The gift of life comes packaged with endless possibilities.

There is much to learn about those potentials.

Some of what we will need to learn will be taught by others.

The depth and complexity of life affirms three certainties:

• Most of what we learn will require effort and sacrifice.

• It will be easier to learn wrong than right.

• There is a cost to what we learn and do not learn.

"Some things cannot be taught; they must be experienced. You never learn the most valuable lessons in life until you go through your own journey." — Roy T. Bennett

Few things we learn will be more vital than one thing.

A curiosity marks brain, fat, gum, muscle, and other cells.

For the most part, we begin life with a set number.

That number does not change.

These cells can grow, shrink, or die, and maybe be replaced.

But their ability to multiply is very limited.

We are well advised to take care of what we have.

For we mostly get just what we get.

"That something is unscientific is not bad; there is nothing the matter with it. It is just unscientific. And scientific is limited, of course, to those things that we can tell about by trial and error." – Richard Feynman

Further bounds are affirmed in our creation.

It is the female gender that brings life to the world.

But this crucial, extraordinary gift comes with a restraint.

Women are born with the eggs they will have for a lifetime.

That limitation is also a stimulation.

Constraint frames our birth.

It turns out it is equally involved in our preservation.

"Unborn lives have a measurable existence that matters – think heartbeat, human features, and a bond to mom." – Author

The favors we receive come matched with a special power.

We get to choose what we do with what we have.

We are free to conserve, build, or nurture.

We are free to waste, destroy, or exploit.

But this power of choice does not come without liability.

We may be free to use our gifts as we wish.

We are not free of the costs linked with that liberty.

"The strongest principle of growth lies in human choice".
– George Eliot

It is a myth that we are all born equal.

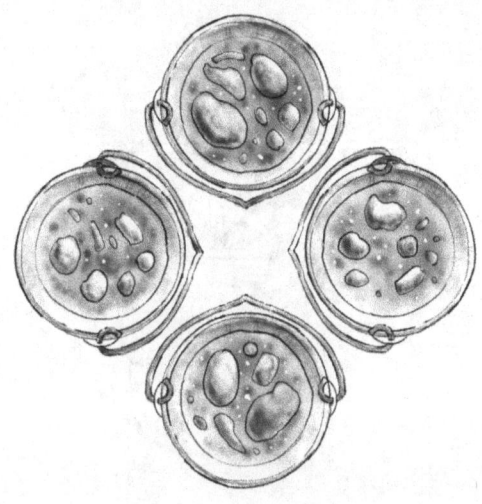

The gifts of life *are not* distributed equally.

In truth, there is only one area in which we are equal:

Our potential to do our best with what we have.

Think about who we should respect most.

Is it those who are naturally gifted?

Or those who face and overcome their limits?

"My turn shall also come: I sense the spreading of a wing."
— Osip Mandelstam, The Selected Poems

We all begin life with a bucket full of undetectable gifts.

Some buckets are big, and some are not so big.

Some may be weaker or hardier than others.

But one thing is never different.

We must be careful with our buckets and what is in them.

Goodness and invincibility do not come in the same package.

"We must all suffer from one of two pains: the pain of discipline or the pain of regret. The difference is discipline weighs ounces while regret weighs tons." – Jim Rohn

For clarity, picture the air we breathe.

By appearance and experience, our supply is limitless.

But with each new measure of pollution, something happens.

What was once clear and crisp becomes hazy and unpleasant.

What once nourished us now begins to poison us.

We need not be perfect in caring for the air or ourselves.

But we must remember good things are *always* perishable.

"In all affairs it's a healthy thing now and then to hang a question mark on the things you have long taken for granted."
– Bertrand Russell

A bounty of goodness is easy to treat casually.

It's easy to imagine an endless stock that will forever be ours.

We can picture those gifts as a limitless credit card.

A card we get to use without interest or repayment.

A better comparison is inheritance from a favored relative.

It is so easy to become reckless with how we use it.

The outcome of that carelessness is predictable.

Once it is gone, it is gone.

"A man who dares to waste one hour of life has not discovered the value of life." – Charles Darwin

Our mouth can reveal the consequence of carelessness.

Neglected and corrupted gum tissue does not renew itself.

Good oral hygiene preserves our gums and teeth.

A mirror tells us that neglect destroys them.

Carelessness with our less obvious gifts is harder to spot.

Unseen things can recede like visible things.

And they don't make false teeth for the inside stuff.

"They're working to bring down the Ministry of Magic from within using a mixture of dark magic and gum disease." —J.K. Rowling

How does something so special exist without a name.

Special things need a name.

All things need a name.

Invisible things especially need a name.

Things with a name are easier to understand.

Unnamed things are more easily lost, misread, or abused.

"If he be Mr. Hyde" he had thought, "I shall be Mr. Seek."
— Robert Louis Stevenson

Chapter Three

Life is Not Easy

There is no such thing as an effortless life.

Some are easier than others, but all living creatures are faced with an insistent reality of stress, pressure, and trials as we make our way through a complex world.

That does not mean that everything is misery and woe. It does mean you have to work at making life a positive experience.

There will always be things coming your way that are especially challenging.

- In Pursuit of Growth -

For a long time, the young man thought his chronic fear and sense of inadequacy were character flaws or a product of a broken nature. That sense of himself lasted for decades.

He put up defenses to protect himself from gnawing feelings of worthlessness, and marveled when others would suggest that he was arrogant or conceited.

He was stuck in a nowhere place. He did not like who he was, but neither did he want to be like others.

Everywhere he looked, he saw dishonesty, immaturity, selfishness, anger, violence, silliness, acting, and greed.

In the end he landed on trying to make himself better. There were very few role models he could embrace, but he did learn that he could pick and choose from other people's examples. He was free to clasp their good that worked and ignore or discard their bad that did not.

Over time – a lot of time – he slowly but surely crafted an identity that he valued and liked.

He thought about the choice between having an artificial and naively high self-esteem, or building one that was real. He realized the latter was better. Just as that which is earned is better than that which is given or stolen.

There was that one word – grow – that relentlessly followed his thoughts and actions. While so many people he knew chose to coast or stop, he kept going.

How grateful he is today for that grace and opportunity...

The gift of existence is *always* challenging.

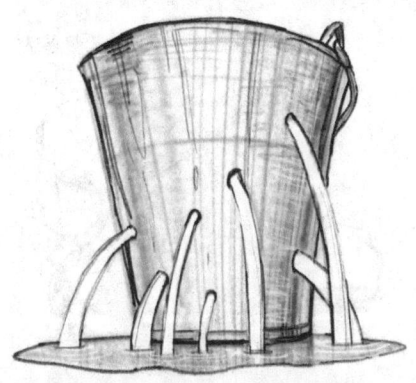

That reality can lead us to that which looks good, but is not.

We can easily confuse what *feels* good with what *is* good.

That's important because all shortcuts hold a hidden cost.

We must pay for them out of our own bucket.

Over time, an abused bucket develops leaks.

And a bucket full of holes is not really a bucket at all.

"I will no longer mutilate and destroy myself in order to find a secret behind the ruins." — Hermann Hesse

In our search for softness, we can find just the opposite.

There are so many things with the power to tempt and trap.

These things can be pleasurable things like:

Wealth | *Power* | *Drugs* | *Lust*

Or not-so-fun things like:

Isolation | *Worry* | *Anger* | *Fear*

These things are marked by an easy start and a hard ending.

Thus, they silently drain us.

They are limitless, and they are very good at what they do.

"Life is hard, but we make it much harder." — Ryan Holiday

Life's hard spots are revealed by one certain thing.

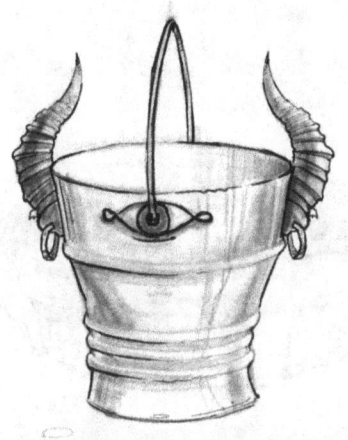

They work extra hard to slow, cancel, defeat, and ingest us.

That is because softness is a resented treasure.

And so, the living are faced with a bitter struggle:

The hard things of life always seek to destroy the soft.

That is because the hard draws energy from this rivalry.

We must decide which side we work for.

"The evil creates for those under their dominion a miniature sick society." — M. Scott Peck

This universal friction between soft and hard is relentless.

But there are revealing differences between the two.

Hardness is limitless and easy.

Softness is limited and demanding.

Hardness takes, while softness gives.

But most curiously, the hard isn't always strong.

And the soft is rarely truly weak.

"Love's weaknesses are better than hate's strengths."
— M. Dhliwayo

Hard things and soft things can look the same on the outside.

In that way, hard things are like beautiful poison berries.

They are soft at first, but they are hard at the end.

Soft things are the opposite.

They are often covered in thorns.

They seem harder, but in the end, they are easier.

And we must choose between the two – all the time.

If that choice is easy, it is probably not the right choice.

"But he who dares not grasp the thorn, should never crave the rose."
— Anne Bronte

There are countless kinds of hard things.

Many are addictive and they are revealed by that trait.

An addiction is anything repeatedly crowding out normalcy.

We can become addicted to just about anything.

And people easily can have more than one addiction.

People in personal pain are extra vulnerable to addiction.

"The attempt to escape from pain, is what creates more pain."
— Gabor Maté

Pain is a natural part of life.

It can come at us through our head, heart, body, or spirit.

In a big, hard world, there are lots of veiled sources of harm.

It is thus easy to get kidnapped by the influences of cynicism.

Thankfully, the world holds more good things than bad.

It is deceiving because the bad stands out.

Concentrating on what is broken does not protect us.

"Life is either a daring adventure or nothing at all." — Helen Keller

Pain pushes us to moan, resent, grieve, submit, or blame.

But we can also choose to respond with learning and growth.

And sometimes we advance more from pain than comfort.

Moments of misery are thus part of life for a reason.

No one can escape stress or the pain that comes our way.

But we have lots of control over how we face both.

"I would not have traded the delights of my suffering for anything in the world." — Gabriel García Márquez

We are granted the liberty to stay stuck in our miseries.

We are equally free to grow through our misfortunes.

Some of life's best teachers can be life's worst moments.

We face a choice every day we live.

We can mourn and surrender or face and overcome.

These are our *only* two stress response options.

"I've learned from experience that the greater part of our happiness or misery depends on our disposition and not on our circumstances."
— Martha Washington

We all have demons, hurdles, and burdens.

That's because nature reveals five clear things:

• We must *all* do battle with our torments.

• No one can relieve us of this responsibility.

• The best sources of relief come from within.

• Pitifulness does not attract rest, respect, or relief.

• Life produces growth and depth out of our struggles.

Hard times are inevitable — hard endings are not.

"I decry the injustice of my wounds, only to look down and see that I am holding a smoking gun in one hand and a fistful of ammunition in the other." — Craig D. Lounsbrough

How we face hardship determines the impact of hardship.

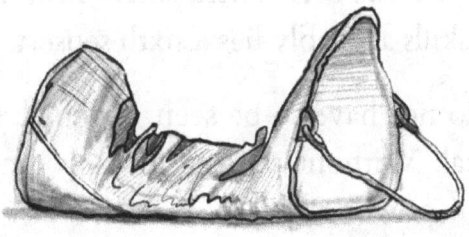

It is prudent to acknowledge trauma's harsh touch.

But we must never be willing to let it define us.

The world is filled with hunger, dirt floors, and hardship.

Too many have prevailed for any of us to submit to ours.

There are no exemptions from the charge to rise up.

And facing hardships always make us stronger.

"I find nothing so singular in life as that everything appears to lose its substance the instant one actually grapples with it."
— Nathaniel Hawthorne

Chapter Four
Soft Spots

We like things we can see, touch, smell, hear, and taste. Beneath those tangible skills arguably lies a sixth sense.

Good things do not have to be seen, touched, smelled, heard, or tasted to be real. Without the use of tools that identify, clarify, and channel, the power of the atom is invisible.

There are many things in your world that require a bigger microscope. That does not mean they do not exist, just that your powers of perception are naturally limited.

And so it is with your *soft spots*. They are too often discovered only when you feel the impact of their absence.

This book is a microscope of sorts. It is intended to help you know more about something that resists discovery, and to help you turn the hidden power of that sixth sense into something special.

– When It is Gone –

Vietnam provided his starkest lessons on the relentless relationship between choice and consequence.

Everything was intense. When the sun shined, it shined hard. When the rain came, it rained hard. When the darkness descended, it was the hardest of blacks. That intensity did something to people.

There was the helicopter crew chief who was about to complete his fifth combat tour. Five thousand helicopters met a violent end in Vietnam. His friend was in his late-twenties, but looked forty. He may have made it home, but he left behind things that he could not replace.

Addicts were legion in Vietnam. Heroin, speed, and acid were cheap and available. Speed captured one of his hooch mates. Before they took him, his light and youth were gone.

His interpreter was forty and looked sixty. His people lived hard and died young. Montagnard's were surrounded by enemies on both sides, and their American allies were about to leave. His tiredness and age were formed in a stew of old harms and an understanding of new ones to come.

Too many approached their tour of duty as an endurance contest. They thus became self-serving islands devoted to one mission – the pursuit of pleasure. That dedication cemented bad habits that would chase them for a lifetime.

The life force of all these men was depleted by internal and external forces. The outcome was the same. Something was lost that was unseen but crucial, and seemingly irreparable.

He wanted to find out what that was…

It is hard to understand something that is invisible.

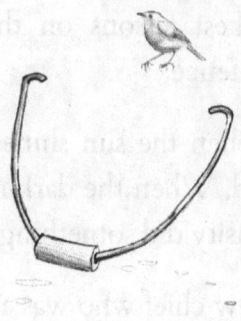

But in each of us are these little special somethings.

We can't see them.

We can't touch them.

We can't hear them, smell them, or taste them.

But if we try really hard, we can feel them.

"How alive is thought, invisible, yet without thought there is no sight."
— Dejan Stojanovic

They are called *softspots*.

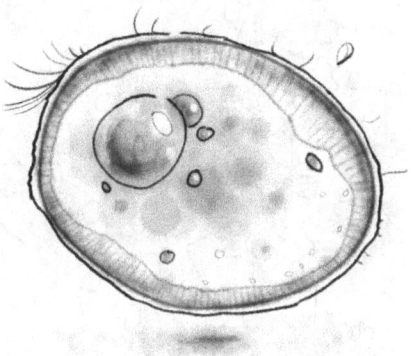

And they are remarkable.

And powerful.

And precious.

And delicate.

And crucial.

"Nothing is softer or more flexible than water, yet nothing can resist it."
– Lao Tzu

Defining something that cannot be seen is difficult.

It is like sharing the details of last night's dream.

It is easy for important things to get lost in the translation.

But there is one way we can try to do it.

Think of a puzzle with many pieces.

We have to put the puzzle together to see what it is about.

This puzzle starts with fifteen pieces.

"I smiled back and I thought how incredible that was, that they would find the time to smile. There was goodness in the world still, even if you couldn't always see it." —Jenny Valentine

Soft spots are brimming with **energy**!

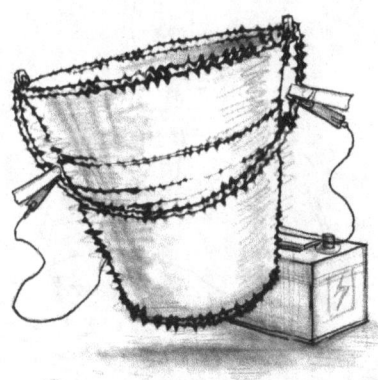

At the core of any effort must be the vitality to get it done.

That is as surely true of doing bad as well as doing good.

Soft spots are made for doing good things.

When applied to good things, they surge and brighten.

When misused to do bad things, the opposite happens.

Soft spots speak in a whisper.

"Take care of us and we will take care of you."

"If you want to find the secrets of the universe, think in terms of energy, frequency and vibration." — Nikola Tesla

Soft spots are fountains of **hope**!

They know we need bridges of hope over our hardships.

Hope knows that however bad something is, it can get better.

Without hope, our challenges can seem overwhelming.

Soft spots partner with hope like strings partner to balloons.

Without them, hope quietly drifts out of reach.

"I don't think of all the misery, but of the beauty that still remains."
— Anne Frank

Soft spots are nourishment for **love**!

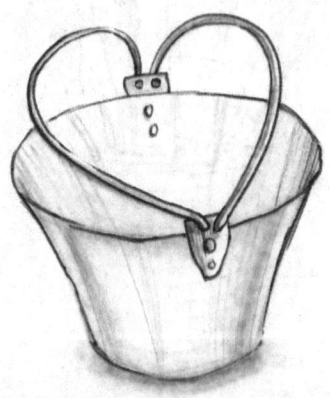

Without love, the darkness would quickly envelope us all.

Love is what we do for the betterment of self and others.

It's a doing kind of thing more than a feeling kind of thing.

Without *soft spots*, love is easily lost amidst the chaos.

"Love all, trust a few, do wrong to none." — William Shakespeare

Soft spots are fountains of **creativity!**

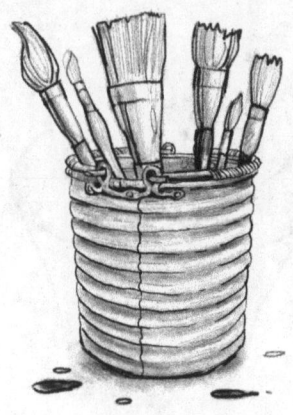

For most of us, creativity is a skill versus a natural talent.

And that skill is not just for the arts.

It is for problem solving, building, and other good things.

The extraordinary power of creativity is often overlooked.

Soft spots stimulate and unleash that power.

Their loss has a way of crushing it.

"Around here, however, we don't look backwards for very long. We keep moving forward, opening up new doors and doing new things, because we're curious...and curiosity keeps leading us down new paths."
— Walt Disney

Soft Spots magnify our *joy!*

It is not news that happiness is an important human need.

We cannot always be joyful, but we can earn our fair share.

Soft spots bubble with joy seeking to be unleashed.

But when we get greedy with our fair share, problems begin.

Attempting to steal joy is like robbing one's own safe.

True, lasting, and renewable joy is a byproduct of balance.

"One can never consent to creep when one feels an impulse to soar."
— Helen Keller

Soft spots are a bedrock of ***patience***!

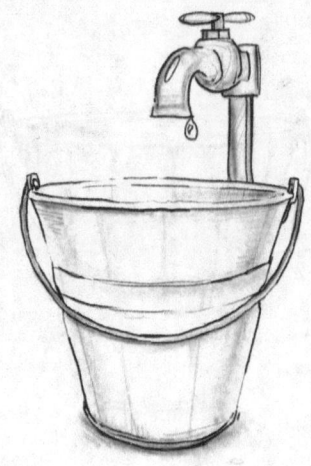

Like creativity, patience is a skill, not a natural talent.

And like all other skills, it can be learned.

A life lived softly is more naturally patient.

Our *soft spots* help make it so.

They understand the rhythm of the world and our life on it.

They give us a tempo for our walk through the moments.

"Rivers know this: there is no hurry. We shall get there some day."
— A.A. Milne

Soft spots are the bridge to *faith*!

They serve as direct testimony to the supernatural.

The supernatural cannot be seen with our natural senses.

Just like *soft spots*.

Spiritual faith commands we reach deeper to stretch higher.

They call it a 'leap of faith' for a reason.

Our *soft spots* uplift us with spring and support as we jump.

"The soul's hands carry the heart's burdens." — Matshona Dhliwayo

Soft spots are generators of ***generosity***!

That is because their gifts stimulate a natural desire to share.

Passing it forward gifts receivers *and* givers.

There are times when we need something we do not have.

Soft spots nudge us to the 'let go' that is so crucial to charity.

That clarifies why the selfish, slack, and careless give little.

"Remember that the happiest people are not those getting more, but those giving more." – H. Jackson Brown Jr.

Soft spots create ***character***!

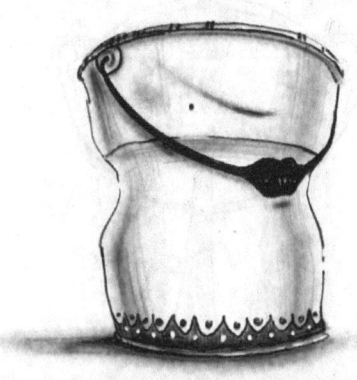

Character is never found or given – it is built and earned.

Character is baked out of a recipe of traits and actions.

It relies on the seven virtues over the seven vices.

Being a character is not the same thing as having character.

The first is quick to embrace darker arts.

The second seeks the light.

"Confront the dark parts of yourself, and work to banish them with illumination and forgiveness. Your willingness to wrestle with your demons will cause your angels to sing." — August Wilson

Soft spots compel ***courage***!

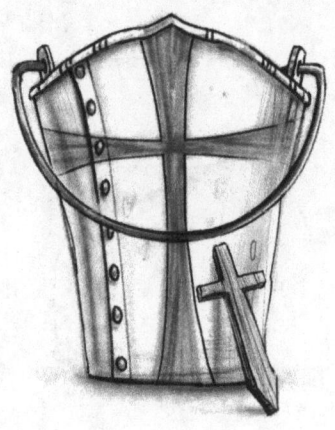

Our hard world obliges that we fight for what is right.

It is necessary to note that courage is not an absence of fear.

It is simply a willingness to press through fear and act.

Goodness requires more bravery than badness.

And *soft spots* give us strength even when we feel weak.

Most good is achieved by those who step over weakness.

"He who is not every day conquering some fear has not learned the secret of life." — Shannon L. Alder

Soft spots are forces for ***frugality***!

Extravagance and waste by some can end in lack for others.

Bounty is a blessing to be valued and properly applied.

Negligence can lead us to hard places.

Frugality is not about being *stingy* with what we have.

It is about being sensible with what we have.

"By sowing frugality, we reap liberty, a golden harvest." – Agesilaus.

Soft spots are nurturers for **compassion**!

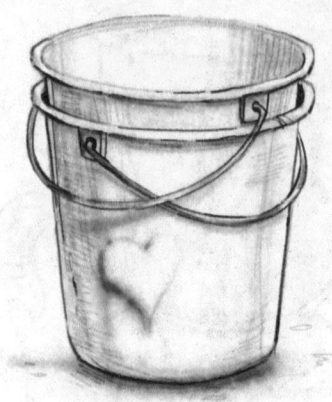

Compassion finds us engaged with the fate of others.

It knows the bell tolls for us all, and we are in life together.

Compassion finds us seeking to uplift, nurture, and assist.

That is important because we all need help sometimes.

Soft spots care for us as a model of how to care for others.

"Be kind, for everyone you meet is fighting a harder battle." — Plato

Soft spots are a stabilizer for **balance**!

Life is a constant effort to juggle conflicting priorities.

Some of those priorities are good – others may not be.

The mission is to not let the bad things pull us off our feet.

To make sure good things do not crowd out other good.

A life of balance does not happen naturally or permanently.

Every day finds us on a tightrope needing our full attention.

"Life is always either a tightrope or a feather bed. Give me the tightrope." – Edith Wharton

Soft spots light the path to **liberation**!

Liberation is one of the most essential blessings in life.

A captured head, heart, hand, or spirit loses its luster.

We live in an insecure world that seeks to control, not grow.

There are always those seeking to constrain.

Liberated spirits ignore that seductive calling.

We must always strive to escape toward freedom's potentials.

"Those who do not move, do not notice their chains."
— Rosa Luxemburg

Soft spots work for the **positive**, the **decent**, and the **helpful**.

This is rarely the natural path of the world at large.

Negativity, immorality, and self-service are tempting.

We are not in charge of this world, nor does it run us.

We are the ultimate source of our landing in life.

The fifteen dedications just mentioned offer clues on how.

> "You are only a bad person if you do bad things. That's not an acquittal. The counterpoint is that you are only a good person if you do good things." — Joseph Fink

Chapter Five
The Theft

It is a confusing conflict in life that hard things are easy to find, but difficult to escape, while soft things are harder to find, and easier to escape.

At times it feels like there is a natural force at work constantly elevating and polishing that which is harmful, as it seeks to constrain and hide that which uplifts.

It is precisely so. Be it by coincidence or design, your world is clearly governed by deceiving forces that, with or without your permission and participation, wish you harm.

Too often and too late, these forces of mischief reveal themselves only by their impact.

There is value in forewarning.

– What Matters –

The journey toward proving his worth was born out of an early pattern of rejection.

Thereafter, he spent much of his life struggling mightily to demonstrate to himself and everyone else that he mattered. Soft moments are illusive when one is caught in the endless circle of escaping doubt through fleeting affirmation.

Success became little more than a short-lived fix. Even the best moments were something to race through in anticipation of the next moment – the next achievement.

The man grew older, but there was no rest. No matter how many accomplishments, self-worth never stuck. His days were a blur; happiness and peace were always temporary.

His mind seemed forever trapped in echoes of rejections, condemnations, and reproaches of his childhood. His joy remained hostage to the need to prove what had in fact, long ago been demonstrated but never recognized.

It took years to understand the truth of achievement, acceptance, and success. There was a dawning recognition that securing man's favor was a hollow victory.

The new mission became to be true to self and the inner values that held tangible worth.

He was a child of God graced with the gift of life. That was enough. He was grateful. He came to understand that all the rest was an illusion...

Soft spots are breakable.

There is a reason.

Imagine pleasure that is endless and without consequence.

What would confine our appetites?

Addiction to our escapes of choice would capture us all.

Fading *soft spots* can warn us of these self-inflicted hazards.

"Real dishes break. That's how you know they're real."
— Marty Rubin

Our *soft spots* do not travel in time.

They do not survive the foggy maze of an uncertain future.

They do not exist in the clouded memories of the past.

Soft spots live in the moment – *right now*. So must we.

Time traveling is an effortless temptation.

But it is never free.

Peace of mind, heart, hand, and spirit die on that journey.

"Happiness, not in another place but this place…not for another hour, but this hour." — Walt Whitman

Human minds are bullies.

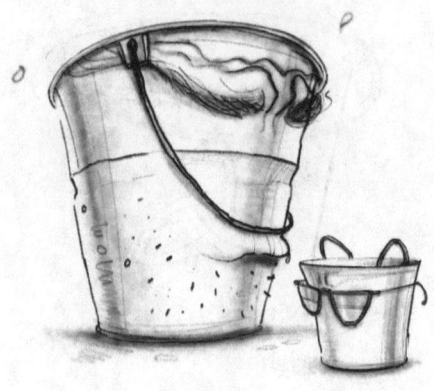

They like to run the show.

And they don't care who they hurt in that mission.

Ironically, the one most hurt is the mind's host.

Humans easily prey on themselves.

We forget that brains drain just like batteries.

"To think too much is a disease." — Dostoyevsky

Curiously, the heart operates much like a garbage disposal.

It can process both pleasant and unpleasant emotions.

Both have something to teach us.

We have to experience both to keep our life in balance.

But humans like to limit ourselves to pleasant feelings.

That bias leads to an accumulation of darker emotions.

They congeal into depression, anxiety, and despair.

"But feelings can't be ignored, no matter how unjust or ungrateful they seem." — Anne Frank

We live on a planet that requires we work and be useful.

Some prefer to relax and do as little as possible.

We dream of retirement, easy jobs, or winning the lottery.

We envision a life of less toil as a life of greater pleasure.

Nothing could be further from the truth.

Most everything that is good requires action and effort.

When we stop moving, we snuff out our own light.

"To learn and not to do is really not to learn. To know and not to do is really not to know." — Stephen R. Covey

The clutter and chatter of a busy world can be captivating.

The sound of the ocean, a bird, or wind is easily displaced.

If what we see and hear can be lost, what of the unclear?

Human spirituality is thus more easily forgotten than found.

This is a monumental mistake.

Without a guide and a sincere moral roadmap, we are lost.

"The doctrines of Christianity, or the many different theologies, are less true than the true myth because they are only attempts to translate the story, while God has expressed it all more adequately in the real incarnation, crucifixion, and resurrection." – C.S. Lewis

Our world is filled with unhappy people.

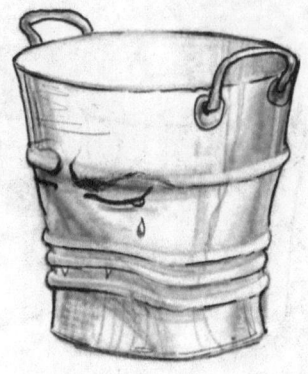

Funny thing about unhappy people:

They like company, and if they cannot find it, they create it.

A good term for such people is *energy vampires*.

They thrive on draining other people's *soft spots*.

Light reminds them of their darkness, and they resent that.

"The baby bat screamed out in fright, 'Turn on the dark, I'm afraid of the light.'" — Shel Silverstein

Sleep is to people what rechargers are to batteries.

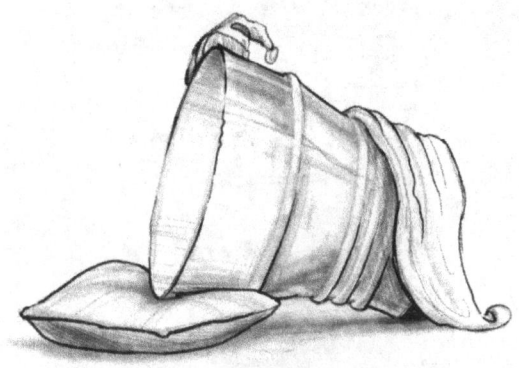

We live in a world of uncharged sleepyheads.

Relentless worry, fear, pressure, and technology make it so.

It helps to learn that sleep is our brain's windshield wiper.

Good sleep cleans off the gunky stuff.

Without it, *soft spots* get tangled in our own mental debris.

> "I've always envied people who sleep easily. Their brains must be cleaner, the floorboards of the skull well swept, all the little monsters closed up in a steamer trunk at the foot of the bed."
> — David Benioff

Soft spots thrive in the company of people.

Like almost all living creatures, we are designed to be social.

We need *people food* as surely as other foods.

People anchor us, nurture us, teach us, and challenge us.

Without adequate people food, we harden inside.

In fact, we cannot truly live without other people.

"Personal relationships are the fertile soil from which all advancement, all success, all achievement in real life grows." – Ben Stein

The body we come in is like a car.

It requires maintenance.

This is not to say the body cannot run without proper care.

It is to say that it will not run well without proper care.

Maintenance includes sleep, nutrition, exercise, and hygiene.

Soft spots need a healthy place to live and grow ill without it.

"If you are in a bad mood, go for a walk. If you are still in a bad mood, go for another walk." — Hippocrates

Chapter Six
Taking Care

Like all good things, *soft spots* require care and maintenance.

You must thus exert caution as you walk through your days. Your choices hold the power to help or to harm.

It is not always clear which is which. For most people, it takes practice, time, and trial and error to determine what serves best and worst.

It is like salt. The same substance that can melt a frozen highway can also cause a car to rust. It is not just the what of things that matter, but also the where, how, and when.

- Life Well Lived -

His grandfather lived to be ninety-six. He was a minister, a builder, a house painter, and a peerless checker player. He was deep and unique.

He was a product of the depression. One of the bone-bending ways he fed his family was logging locust trees and cutting them into railroad ties with a broad axe and a crosscut saw.

The boy's grandfather lost his father and brother when he was young. Both died as a consequence of a train wreck on a mountain curve in a remote part of North Carolina. Not many years after, he too almost died from the influenza epidemic of nineteen-eighteen.

He was wild in his youth – prone to anger and in matters of conflict, quick to use his fists. Called to the ministry in his thirties, his anger faded and he studied the Bible relentlessly. His knowledge, example, and sincerity shined in the pulpit.

Sadly, he left this world still doubting himself. If only he could have realized what others saw and loved. He was one of those people who started out hard and landed soft. His was a model of a soul that sweetened with time. He learned how to press on regardless and lived most of his life in pain as he worked to ease it in others...

There are some things that place *soft spots* at special risk.

We live in a world filled with harmful influences.

Those harms can exist within or without.

Some are controllable, and some are not.

Amidst the threats, caution is necessary to keep our balance.

It is extraordinarily easy to fall prey to a fallen planet.

"Ours is a world of nuclear giants and ethical infants." – Omar Bradley

Trauma can harm our _soft spots_.

Extra-harsh exposures have a hard impact.

Picture a car running into a tree.

Both the tree and the car will be damaged.

Some traumas have short impacts, while others last longer.

Before we begin the repair, we must recognize the damage.

There is a giant difference in impact and permanent harm.

"God wants you to be delivered from what you have done and from what has been done to you - both are equally important to Him."
— Joyce Meyer

Empaths have especially vulnerable *soft spots*.

An empath is a person with exceptional sensitivity.

That depth of feeling creates power and vulnerability.

Picture a fair-skinned person at the beach in the noon sun.

Without sunscreen, they are easily burned.

Empaths have to make sure to put on their heart-screen.

"The less defined our sense of self is and the more toxic energy we take on from others, the more we are prone to losing touch with our Souls."
— Aletheia Luna

Complexity can lead to soft spot vulnerability.

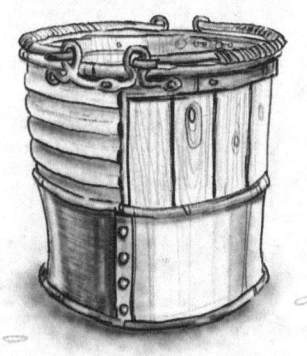

We begin life with a head, heart, hand, and spirit.

We have all four, but are not necessarily strong in all four.

Those who are face a daily internal battle.

Such people are called *One Percenters*.

They have to work hard to stay stable in an unstable world.

"The mission is to turn our unintended and confusing burdens into much intended and astonishing blessings." — Author

Cultural influences can corrupt our *soft spots*.

Mankind may be created equal, but cultures are not.

No culture is perfect, but some are darker than others.

They gag liberty, opportunity, responsibility, and prosperity.

These things are the foundation of human potential.

Healthy cultures are not created or preserved by accident.

They are dependent on wisdom, service, and courage.

"Civilizations die from suicide, not by murder." — Arnold Toynbee

Stress is a *soft spot* killer.

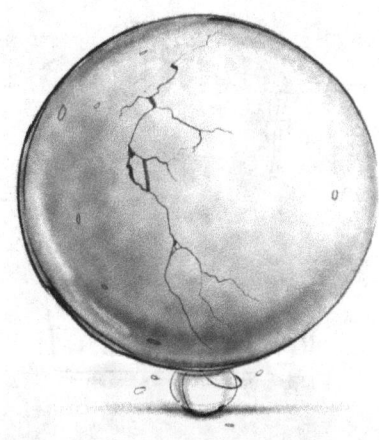

Circular stress is particularly lethal.

Linear stress has a beginning, a middle, and an end.

That is the normal stress that comes into every life.

Circular stress finds us stuck in a loop.

We cannot find answers, solutions, or a way out.

Circular stress is like a circular saw that cuts us into pieces.

"We all live in a house on fire, no fire department to call; no way out, just the upstairs window to look out of while the fire burns the house down with us trapped, locked in it." — Tennessee Williams

Bad role models can cast a shadow on our *soft spots*.

We live on a difficult planet.

There is no way to figure out everything by ourselves.

We have to learn from others.

Bad examples are a toxin that slowly poisons.

Except when we use them as examples of what *not* to be.

Good examples of how to live right are indispensable.

"Children have never been very good at listening to their elders, but they have never failed to imitate them." —James Baldwin

Persisting **powerlessness** overpowers our *soft spots*.

Power is not bad – it all depends on what we do with it.

If we seek to pursue the good in life, power is imperative.

Without it, we will feel and be helpless and feeble.

Helpless and feeble are not the way we are intended to be.

Besides, powerless is almost always an illusion.

There is a way around, over, under, or through most hurdles.

"Power does not corrupt. Fear corrupts... perhaps the fear of a loss of power." — John Steinbeck

Abuse batters our *soft spots* into broken pieces.

There is a difference between hardship and abuse.

We all have hard moments from hard people or hard events.

Abuse is purposeful, damaging, and inescapable exploitation.

It can come from family, predators, and authority figures.

The list of potential abusers is endless.

Our efforts to escape abuse must also be endless.

And a little bit more.

"Many survivors insist they're not courageous: 'If I were courageous, I would have stopped the abuse...If I were courageous, I wouldn't be scared. You don't start with courage and then face fear. You become courageous because you face your fear." — Laura Davis

Dependency takes our *soft spots* captive.

There is nothing wrong with needing help and support.

It is *counting* on help and support that gets us into trouble.

Two things happen with excessive dependency.

Both sides are tempted into misusing one another.

We reliably resent those upon whom we are dependent.

Life is best traveled when walked mostly on our own feet.

"It is this dependency that became, and is, the breeding ground for abuses of power." — Bell Hooks

Chapter Seven

Replenishment

Like so many good things in life, *soft spots* are geared more to care and conservation than repair and replacement.

What you misuse, you can easily lose.

There are a few exceptions, but they come with a price. False teeth are better than no teeth, but they are not quite as good as real teeth.

When you miss the mark on taking good care of your *soft spots*, there are things you can do to make up for some of the loss.

The wisdom of the past holds some answers on how.

- Pepper -

He found her in a newspaper ad and they first met in a convenience store parking lot. The owner had brought two siblings in a travel crate and offered him his choice. The female, the smaller of the two, caught his attention.

Pepper was an English Setter. She was smart, loving, energetic, and dedicated to her primary vocation – hunting.

Pepper would hunt anything. Though she preferred game birds, she would willingly substitute crows, pigeons, sparrows, and hummingbirds if circumstances allowed. She also embraced the prey-like suitability of lizards, frogs, rabbits, squirrels, bugs, bees, moths, and shadows.

From the beginning they went to work together. Every day Pepper would jump in the car, take her seat, and immediately begin scanning the horizon for trackable fare.

Black and white with a dark left eye and a cowlick, like all dogs, she was special and pretty. And she was fun. There was always something going on with Pepper. Tug-of-war, tag, and laser chasing were favorites.

Pepper left an inerasable imprint. He had known many great dogs over the course of his life. Lane, Beth, TB, Abby, and Domino all created a permanent pawprint on his memory. But none were quite like Pepper.

Perhaps it was their constant companionship at, to, and from work. Perhaps it was their thirty-minute daily run. Mostly it was just that Pepper was special. Those eyes could read your mind, heart, and soul. She was a timely *soft spot*.

She blessed him with unparalleled grace...

A guy named Solomon had solid ideas on replenishment.

At the end of a grand life, he found himself feeling empty.

He recognized he had been careless with himself and others.

He traced his many errors to one word – *vanity*.

In pursuit of the world's passions, he had spent his vitality.

In one of his books in the Bible, he provides clarification.

Ecclesiastes highlights his errors and antidotes to self-harm.

"Vanity, thy name is vampire." —Jim Butcher

Solomon's advice can be counted on the fingers of one hand.

It was his belief there were five exemptions to life's vanities.

In his latter days, he was able to simplify the human script.

Not coincidently, his advice couples directly to *soft spots*.

His wish was to address our wellbeing on earth and beyond.

His hand of advice points to five crucial elements:

Laboring, Loving, Learning, Living, and Listening.

"Confront the dark parts of yourself, and work to banish them with illumination and forgiveness. Your willingness to wrestle with your demons will cause your angels to sing." — August Wilson

Labor is about work.

Good work is the investment of our gifts in useful action.

Work is not easy.

Few things that are good are simultaneously effortless.

Work feeds, connects, challenges, and keeps us busy.

Doing something with ourselves is a matchless energizer.

"*Action may not always bring happiness, but there is no happiness without action.*" — William James

Love is medicine for the head, heart, hand, and spirit.

It works on self and others.

But it is not always an easy medicine to swallow.

Love requires we turn away from our selfish gratifications.

The magic of love is subtle and slow versus clear and quick.

Love is a healing agent for all that ails us and our world.

We will find many things to learn in our lifetime.

The greatest of these will be our efforts to love and be loved.

"Darkness cannot drive out darkness: only light can do that. Hate cannot drive out hate: only love can do that." – Martin Luther King

Our brain's capacity to *learn* is infinite for a reason.

With learning comes wisdom, and with wisdom comes truth.

Finding and standing on truth is one of life's hard challenges.

There are so many things that seem truthful, but are not.

Relentless learning gets us ever closer to truth.

There is great comfort and health in living as a sponge.

Some learning is natural, but the best is pursued as treasure.

"For me, I am driven by two main philosophies: know more today about the world than I knew yesterday and lessen the suffering of others. You'd be surprised how far that gets you." — Neil Tyson

We were placed on earth to *live* with intention.

Our life is a gift, but like most gifts, it comes with a price.

Life is a process of endless investment of self.

One important investment is that of gratitude.

In the face of hardships, it is easy to resent versus value life.

People who praise life are happier, softer, and more at peace.

Life must be lived in wise celebration, not bitter endurance.

"Because you are alive, everything is possible." – Thich Nhat Hanh

The last one – to **listen** – is the toughest of all.

For most of us, the spiritual side of life is confusing.

It requires a leap of faith not natural to the human condition.

Within us is a voice that calls on us to listen and follow.

We have to hush and use a deeper ear to hear that call.

In that listening, we can find a matchless compass.

"With your permission and cooperation, God will work the soil of your heart, and your life will become a lovely garden for him."
— Linda Evans Shepherd

Chapter Eight
A Simple Script

Amidst the complexities of life, confusion is the rule more often than the exception. There are so many conflicting tugs and seductions on what is right and wrong, and good and bad, that stumbling into traps is frighteningly easy.

One way to shine the light on the differences between goodness and darkness is a simple but particularly powerful life formula containing just fourteen parts.

The wisdom of the ages, and our futures, are contained therein. Who would have thought that an effective life script can be found in just fourteen words?

- No Escape -

There was sorrow in his patient's story. It began with his first exposure to a hidden path, one that led to moments of peace from a seemingly magic substance. A plant birthed to the kiss of a flame.

The alluring smoke brought with it heretofore unknown rest. It came quickly and quietly, as it gave everything and asked nothing.

At first it was a random opportunity made sweeter by infrequency. Each fresh opportunity was met with a growing dose of anticipatory expectation.

The ready availability of a sanctuary was comforting – the relief, even more so. It was a ring that could be worn or laid aside as need demanded.

Over time something happened. When challenges arose, so did desire for relief in its newly learned best form. The human means to coping were seemingly too difficult, too complex, and too slow.

The ending was not like the beginning. Not knowing that character and strength must be tested to grow, the young person's identity and joy faded at a time it was meant to bloom.

His heart and hope were lost in the smokey haze. Too late he learned that most demons wear a mask.

Soft spots do not survive amidst stolen bliss...

The Seven Vices

There are certain forces and activities that are venomous.

That toxicity applies to both the giver and the receiver.

Dependably, these things are easy to master and deploy.

They are so common as to sometimes seem normal.

Poison ivy's proliferation does not reveal its toxicity.

Vice squeezes the life out of life.

"There is not a crime, there is not a dodge, there is not a trick, there is not a swindle, there is not a vice which does not live by secrecy."
— Joseph Pulitzer

Pride is a baseless appraisal of our merit, clout, and rights.

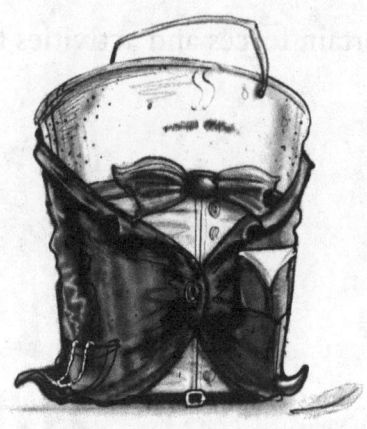

Pride assumes our wings can fly high without higher effort.

Pride is distinct from being proud of one's ability or actions.

Pride is artificial and arrogant – *proud* is real and modest.

Pride does not listen or learn.

Pride runs over its own feet, as well as everyone in its way.

And at the end of pride's path is a cliff.

"A proud man is always looking down on things and people; and, of course, as long as you are looking down, you cannot see something that is above you." — C.S. Lewis

Laziness has the goal of high pleasure with low effort.

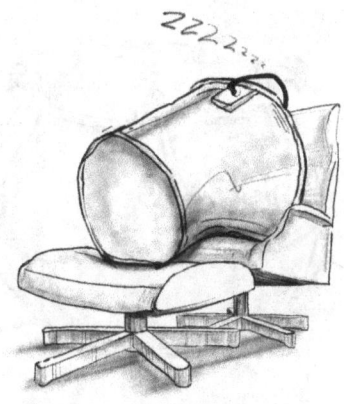

Most things that are good require us to put forth energy.

Laziness pretends otherwise and attempts to pilfer comfort.

Relaxing is recharging – laziness is draining.

All runners rest after they race.

The lazy seek to skip the race altogether.

The best of life requires investment.

Bank accounts without deposits will soon be empty.

"Stay away from lazy parasites, who perch on you just to satisfy their needs, they do not come to alleviate your burdens, hence, their mission is to distract, detract and extract, and make you live in abject poverty."
— Michael Bassey Johnson

Gluttony is the addictive pursuit of excess.

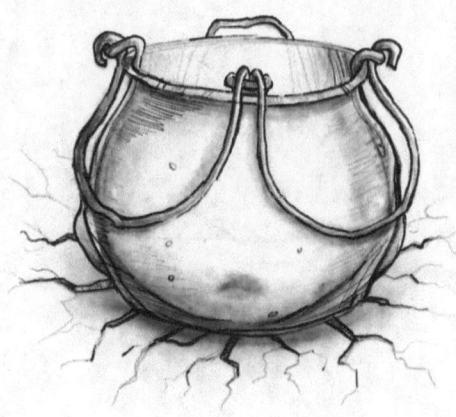

Gluttons run on the premise that more is always better.

If one glass of wine is fine, a whole bottle would be better.

Like all addictions, gluttony leads to behavioral blindness.

It does not matter what our appetites pursue.

Extremes in power, pleasure, food, drugs, etc. consume.

The weight of gluttony crushes the glutton.

"He who is not contented with what he has, would not be contented with what he would like to have." — Socrates

Lust is a kissing cousin of gluttony.

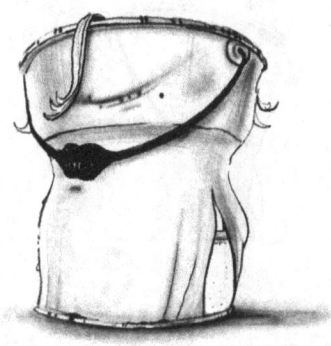

The mission of lust is just a bit more specific – it is about sex.

Like anything that feels good, sex has addictive potentials.

Sex for sex's sake may be fun, but it is also dangerous.

Without the counterbalance of love, it can become a monster.

Lust can easily corrupt our head, heart, hand and spirit.

Sex without love can be like gasoline without a container.

"God made every one of us a sexual being, and that is good. Attraction and arousal are the natural, spontaneous, God-given responses to physical beauty, while lust is a deliberate act of the will." – Rick Warren

Avarice can be boiled down to another word – greed.

In a hard world, greed is an easy temptation.

If a little is good, it seems like more would be better.

Once we turn on that faucet, it is difficult to turn it off.

We are so afraid we will get left out that we become obsessed.

That is what greed really is – an obsession with more.

When we surrender to greed, we damage our *off* button.

Avarice is an itch that cannot be scratched away.

"It was not curiosity that killed the goose who laid the golden egg, but an insatiable greed that devoured common sense." — E.A. Bucchianeri

Envy ignores our gifts while coveting the gifts of others.

No two human beings are alike.

We come with our own unique head, heart, hand, and spirit.

The world helps form us, but it does not own us.

Dwelling on how others look, do, think, or seem is disruptive.

Looking at passing scenery is a mistake while one is driving.

It is good to learn from others. It is a fault to want to be another.

"It is in the character of very few men to honor without envy a friend who has prospered." — Aeschylus

Anger as a habit is like brushing one's teeth with dirt.

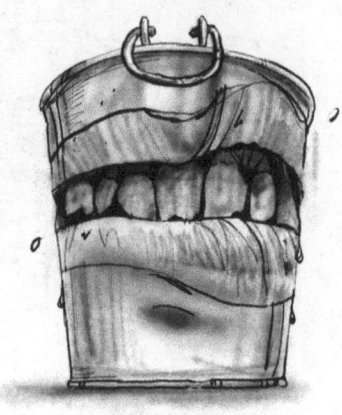

Anger takes good energy and applies it badly.

And anger always lies.

Anger conceals humble emotions like, fear, hurt, or sorrow.

These emotions feel weak, and so we put on angry armor.

It is heavy and gloomy, and makes us impulsive and foolish.

Anger is like the kudzu vine that chokes as it cloaks.

"*Anybody can become angry — that is easy, but to be angry with the right person and to the right degree and at the right time and for the right purpose, and in the right way — that is not within everybody's power and is not easy.*" — Aristotle

The Seven Virtues

Standing in contrast to the seven vices are the seven virtues.

The dissimilarity between these opposing forces is stark.

Whereas vice comes easily, virtue commands resolute effort.

Vice bids the appeal of autonomy, pleasure, and distraction.

Virtue calls with the soft plea of duty and delayed reward.

It is what comes later that most marks their deep divide.

Vice consumes – virtue cultivates.

"The Seven Social Sins are: Wealth without work. Pleasure without conscience. Knowledge without character. Commerce without morality. Science without humanity. Worship without sacrifice. Politics without principle." – Frederick Lewis Donaldson

Chasity is a form of conservation.

It is based in the idea that bodily intimacy is not a casual act.

Sexual restraint is not popular in today's indulgent society.

But popularity rarely affirms a culture is correct in its norms.

In the case of sexuality, we are far more wrong than right.

The emotional and physical have direct neural linkage.

Casual sex pretends some parts are liberated from the whole.

Chastity knows the heart acquires great risk in that pretense.

"Chastity is a difficult long-term matter; one must wait patiently for it to bear fruit for the happiness of loving kindness which it must bring. But at the same time chastity is the sure way to happiness."
– Pope John Paul

Temperance is the act of restraint, moderation, and delay.

Human beings like none of these things.

Each curbs our thirst for plentiful and prompt gratification.

We like getting what we want, when and how we want it.

Temperance suggests there may be better times and ways.

We do not ski in summer or swim in winter for good reasons.

The intemperate believe life is an endless zero-calorie buffet.

"It is a queer thing. In a time of great need, when powerful leadership is demanded, the people—confused and excited—hear only the strident voices of the audacious, and refuse to listen to the voice of wisdom which, being wise, is temperate." — Lloyd C. Douglas

Charity is the act of aid and grace to the less fortunate.

To be the real deal, it must be a gift without kickback.

Recognition and reward corrupt charity into bartering.

But there is a distinct positive pay-off from charity.

What goes around reliably comes around.

The impact is not only what is given, but what is created.

Charity is just *love* in another form.

"No one has ever become poor by giving." — Anne Frank

Diligence is the earnest pursuit of productive activities.

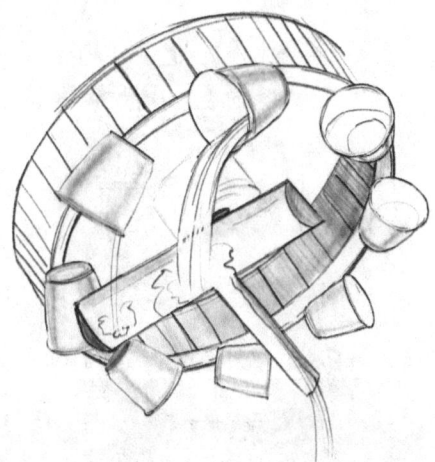

Getting good from life requires putting good things into life.

As we have shared, that is almost always an uphill course.

We live in a world where many seek to do less, not more.

In that world, entitlement is often celebrated over merit.

The diligent refuse this regressive script.

They know the world's dedicated rotations set our example.

"Gardens are not made by singing 'Oh, how beautiful!' and sitting in the shade." — Rudyard Kipling

Patience is the skill of facing trials with grace and dignity.

Those challenges can be internal, external, or both.

The world is relentless in poking our patience.

Consider road rage, profanity, violence, anger, and revenge.

All are evidence of failure.

Patience works to win outside even as it struggles inside.

Feeling inpatient does not require we behave impatiently.

"Patience is bitter, but its fruit is sweet." — Aristotle

Kindness is the effort to treat others with respect and care.

Like charity, kindness is another first-class bridge to love.

The more we practice kindness, the more easily it comes.

The less we practice, the less we see its value.

In a hardening world, kindness is a wonderous remedy.

That is why the forces of darkness move against kindness.

Darkness resents the competitive edge of kindness.

"Three things in human life are important: the first is to be kind; the second is to be kind; and the third is to be kind." — Henry James

Humility is the active pursuit of a modest personal identity.

Humbleness receives more cultural lip service than embrace.

In today's world, the loud and pretentious gain the attention.

And so, we often confuse arrogance with competence.

Self-importance is mostly a shaky cover-up for self-doubt.

Humility is a solid foundation for growth and achievement.

Our world needs steady doers over flamboyant actors.

"True humility is not thinking less of yourself; it is thinking of yourself less." — Rick Warren

Chapter Nine
Hard Spots

Your world brims with temptations, attractions, and seductions seeking to pull you toward darkness. Some of these forces are especially wretched and cursed with the power to harm.

Within their makeup is an extra measure of malignancy sanctioned to ensnare the unwitting, the careless, and those who otherwise sidestep the impact of personal choice in personal outcomes.

These are special poisons that merit your strongest diligence and resistance.

- Retirement -

Forty-five years is a long time. In a profession that is noted for an exceptional rate of burn-out, it is a really long time.

During those forty-five years, he connected with an amazing variety of people facing a host of challenges. Most of those people were good people. Some were not. Some were dedicated to their toxicities, and as a consequence, they did great harm to themselves and others.

He remembers the wife of an unfaithful husband who got so caught up in hating him for his affair that she lost her marriage and her life.

He remembers the wealthy, much celebrated, and powerful community personality who secretly preyed on young girls. He got away with it here; one doubts he was able to hide in the afterlife.

He remembers the person who hid behind dishonesty. Though graced with talent, their gifts were smothered by a parade of lies.

He remembers the young lady whose heart and hope were broken by her chosen guy's pornography obsession. His daily fantasy lost her.

He remembers the young man whose traumatic combat experiences led him to criminal violence. The ghosts of that choice haunt him ruthlessly.

He remembers the patient who was a professional thief. He was good at it and got away with his selfishness right up to the moment his empty soul prompted murder.

He remembers all the families who struggled and cried over loved ones lost to drugs. He mourned a culture who surrendered to the scourge.

He remembers the passive-aggressive personalities who poisoned others with silent violence. Control, negativity, and manipulation are vulturous.

He remembers every narcissistic-sociopath. They were predictably devoted to depleting others and hiding the bodies. Recovery was rare and hard.

He remembers the people who chose to escape through suicide. He saw how they left behind pain for others, and – too often – more than one body.

He came to understand that there are many things that do harm, and some things that do exceptional harm. He saw that these things fester silently in a culture too often blind to evil.

He also remembers the good, courageous, and marvelous things.

He remembers the many single mothers who worked multiple jobs and embraced their children as a responsibility versus a burden.

He remembers the couples in distress who did not treat one another as disposable. They worked hard to salvage their love, instead of pursuing a fantasy restart with a recruited replacement.

He remembers the older people who could very much be taught new tricks and skills and who were often more diligent at such than they ever would have been in younger days.

He remembers the shy, sensitive, self-doubting young people who were ruthlessly preyed upon by institutional bullies. They were easy victims for those dodging personal accountability amidst an education system that prized illusion over truth.

He remembers the many who were seduced by the false promises of psycho-active medications, broke free, and began the work of growing versus temporarily escaping the symptoms of despair.

He remembers those who faced the hardship of giving new life an opportunity to also live.

He remembers so much, that he cannot imagine wanting to stop meeting new people with the same courage to face life head and hands on.

Retirement – no. Far better the joys of refirement...

Hate consumes the hater more surely than the hated.

That is because hate poisons the vessel that holds it.

That is because hate bonds us to those we hate.

That is because hate smothers goodness in and around us.

That is because hate binds us as it blinds us.

That is because hate flings open the door to other evils.

There is no life script that contains peace and hate.

Hate accepts no rivals as it strangles its container.

"I have decided to stick to love...Hate is too great a burden to bear."
— Martin Luther King Jr

Preying is the act of plundering the world around us.

Preying is about abusing and misusing for personal gain.

We may exploit people.

We may exploit our environment.

We may exploit animals.

We may exploit anything, because everything is exploitable.

But all things have limits, and all actions have consequence.

"In the end, by preying on our world, we exploit ourselves too. Then again, that's how the most successful predators work, she thinks ruefully. We stumble into their traps and do their work for them while we're busy getting on with the business of living."
— Kimberly Morgan

Lying is a most common and effortless defense.

No one has to be taught to lie – we are born with this skill.

We use it to evade charge, conflict, or consequence.

There are many problems with lying – addiction is a big one.

The more we lie, the less we recognize it.

Another problem is that nothing good exists without truth.

A bodyguard of lies assassinates those it pretends to protect.

The truth is always an insult or a joke, lies are generally tastier. We love them. The nature of lies is to please. Truth has no concern for anyone's comfort" — Katherine Dunn

Predatory people come in every size, shape, style, and state.

In today's society, many hide behind a victim shield.

One of the more common ruses involves drugs.

Making a decision to try a drug is like careless driving.

If a wreck or addiction results, personal choice led the way.

That power of choice separates *real* and *fake* victims. There is one very reliable way to tell the difference.

Real victims embrace responsibility – fake ones do not.

"Some men just want to watch the world burn." — Christopher Nolan

Pornography is a highly discounted cultural addiction.

Technological advancements have unleashed this harm.

It is easy to obtain, privately available, and essentially free.

Problems abound, beginning with the issue of fidelity.

Most women absorb pornography as concealed adultery.

It also exploits the women recruited to manufacture it.

The kicker is a dopamine fix triggering accelerating craving.

The autopsied brain of a porn addict mirrors a drug addict.

"Young people rely on the Internet and its unlimited supply of pornography to ward off external stress. The instant gratification gratifies instantly. But the external stress is, in large part, being caused by the Internet itself. The Internet itself is a feedback loop; it creates the demand that it then seeks to fill." — A.N. Turner

Violence is an accelerating world phenomenon.

We are hurting one another with intent and proficiency.

Physical violence is the worst of many bad forms of violence.

Child and spouse abusers, gangs, and zealots offer example.

The issue behind violence is power.

There is a high that comes from harming and dominating.

Like all highs, that fix is temporary.

The damage, scars, and accountabilities can last forever.

"In a world gushing blood day and night, you never stop mopping up pain." — Aberjhani

Stealing is fast becoming a permitted harm.

Thieves come as burglars, politicians, shoplifters, captains of industry, entitlement addicts, politicians, and family.

Taking that which is unearned is the common thread.

Most thieves start small and grow bigger.

Like all addictions, stealing stimulates more desire to steal.

A pilfered piece of candy premiers cheating on your taxes.

But no unearned opportunity comes to us without a price.

Every time we steal, a chunk of our soul is sold cheaply.

"Socialism is the belief, therefore, that stealing is acceptable as long as another man or group of men says so." —Joel McDurmon

In the 21st century, **drugs** are a grave source of social harm.

Bad feelings are a stubborn life certainty, and we seek relief.

When used as a counter to this reality, drugs have penalties. One

big impact is that while we are high, we stop growing.

Artificial feelings, thoughts, or actions only mimic progress.

The harms of drugs can be slow and subtle, or fast and hard.

The greater the escape, the greater the harm.

Reality is difficult but rewarding; escapes are easy but costly.

"Drugs are a waste of time. They destroy your memory and your self-respect and everything that goes along with your self-esteem."
— Kurt Cobain

Venting is a common form of stress reduction.

But there is a problem, in that venting does not do that well.

The theory is that getting things out relieves pressure.

What venting mostly does is stimulate and magnify stress.

Venting *can* be useful as a precursor to active change efforts.

We can start by telling others that our grass is too high.

But then we have to get busy mowing that grass.

"There was something peculiarly gratifying about shouting in a blind rage until your words ran out. Of course, the aftermath was less pleasant. Once you'd told everyone you hated them and not to come after you, where exactly did you go?" — Cassandra Clare

Silent violence masks itself behind camouflage.

Examples include control, negativity, and manipulation.

Controlling people choke the life out of those around them.

Negative people dim the lights and pull us into darkness.

Manipulators exploit for personal gain.

Silent violence is as lecherous & treacherous as louder forms.

Hidden cancer can kill just as surely as a gun.

"We hide our demons so good, that the angels we show, bare the shame on their faces." — Anthony Liccione

Narcissism is selfishness in its most malignant form.

Though charming and seductive, narcissists are self-devoted.

They suck the life force out of everyone and everything.

They are most easily tracked by the damage they leave.

Narcissists can change, but very rarely do.

Change is work, and narcissists believe they are exempt.

They prefer to con others into being their worker bees.

When the worker no longer serves, it is cast aside.

"The lion is most handsome when looking for food." —Ru

Self-harm is a selfish act that creates extended damage.

Over the course of life, almost everyone thinks about it.

Life can be sore, and that tempts us to jump ship.

Most people do not want to die; they want relief from agony.

There are better ways to get pain relief than dying.

Suicide has an echo that lingers and haunts our loved ones.

Worse, it opens the door for others to do the same thing.

"But in the end, one needs more courage to live than to kill himself."
— Albert Camus

Chapter Ten

It Takes a Team

It is not news that human beings are complex organisms. What is news is how important it is to make sure your parts receive proper attention so they can be taught to work together.

Your four biggest puzzle pieces are the head, heart, hand, and spirit. All four matter, and all four have a potent influence on the others.

Developing unity among your competing parts is a life-long challenge.

There are some clear steps and skills that can make that journey a lighter and more hopeful commission.

- A Deeper Touch -

He met the gentleman per a suggestion from a friend in graduate school. He will always be grateful for that timely introduction to a source of influence that probably saved his life.

In a world full of characters, this gentleman was one of the most unique. A clinical social worker by profession, he knew more about personal understanding, support, and growth than anyone he had ever met.

It was time for his clinical internship. Outreach to this potential mentor landed that opportunity. It was an unimagined launch to a special ride.

One of his new supervisor's gifts was humor. He was all business helping people, and he worked far harder than most. But he had fun doing it.

On the head, he minced no words, "Half the world happily pretends that mental masturbation is the same thing as reason." "Real thinking is productive. Most of us just go around molesting our brain as a play toy."

His comments on love were a personal revelation and a spark for hope. "Whatever you need, give it," he would say. "All you have to do to feel loved, is to give love to others." That simple but profound suggestion pointed to an escape tunnel out of a stifling prison of loneliness.

When it came to life and what you put your hand to, it was his recommendation to "treat it all responsibly, but never seriously." "The world is too crazy to treat seriously," he shared. "It always has been."

Though skeptical of religious dogma and careless in his application of profanity, his mentor understood the importance of faith. He had absorbed the Bible from beginning to end and used that knowledge to reach people.

Knowing that everything good is grounded in honesty, he highlighted the Bible's reference to the spiritual person as a "truth seeker." He once suggested that most everything he taught his patients came from Ecclesiastes and Proverbs.

This gentleman was far from perfect. Like most complex people, there were gaps in his self-awareness and actions. Though he uplifted far more people than he injured, some of his harms lingered beyond his passing.

He ran a helping model for eighty-plus years until he had a stroke. Ironically, it took the ability to talk away from a man who had spent his life helping people with words as surely as any other tool.

He was with the gentleman shortly before his passing. That kiss he blew still lingers on his mind. Even while approaching death, he was still thinking of others.

What a rare source of unconditional love, guidance, and example he was. Meeting him so soon after the conflicting impact of Vietnam was a Godsend. Per his touch, there was a bridge to a future of hope, meaning, and potential.

Gratitude lingers too...

The Head

Like all things human, the brain is jointly licensed to be a remarkable source of enlightenment and enterprise, or a debilitating source of worry and folly.

Where your brain lands is best determined by a commitment to choice over chance. The brain you fail to manage will inevitably manage you.

Like all things worthy and powerful, the human brain is designed to be your friend. It needs your help to stay in that good place.

The mind is selfish.

It likes to push the rest of us around.

It likes to run things all the time.

It likes to put itself first.

It likes to be in control.

It is about it.

"Shut up, she tells her monkey mind. Please shut up, you picker of nits, presser of bruises, counter of losses, fearer of failures, collector of grievances future and past." — Leni Zumas

Brains come with a built in ON/OFF button.

Sometimes it gets forgotten.

Sometimes it gets rusty.

Sometimes it gets busted.

When it breaks, we get stressed, prickly, and unhappy.

Nothing can be on all the time.

Anything that tries to stay on all the time burns out.

"The tricky thing about rumination is that it feels like it's helpful, but there's no action taken, and you don't move forward to some sort of solution." —Carla Grayson

Turning the brain off is a learned proficiency.

All skills require knowledge, practice, and persistency.

This is especially true of skills applied to the human brain.

That is because most of our brains are spoiled.

Our brains often behave like a tantrum-prone two-year-old.

They want what they want when and how they want it.

We have to teach our brain that we run it – not the reverse.

"Today I escaped anxiety. Or no, I discarded it, because it was within me, in my own perceptions—not outside." – Marcus Aurelius

The process of living requires thought.

But not just thought from instinct, conditioning, or training.

That is how animals think.

Humans have greater complexities in our thoughts.

We can think toward inspiration, wisdom, and achievement.

We also have thoughts devoted to mischief, ego, and malice.

The powers of choice and self-control are thus very critical.

"We are dying from overthinking. We are slowly killing ourselves by thinking about everything. Think. Think. Think. You can never trust the human mind anyway. It's a death trap." — Anthony Hopkins

There are three primary parts to the human brain.

First comes is the frontal cortex, or the *Spock brain*.

Then there is the middle section, or the *Monkey brain*.

Last in the lineup is the back section, or the *Lizard brain*.

The first thinks, the second reacts, and the third just runs.

For many people, the *Monkey brain* is in charge.

That is where the majority of our emotions come from.

That is not the brain section that should be leading the way.

Brain balance finds all three parts working together.

"We can't solve problems by using the same kind of thinking we used when we created them." — Albert Einstein

Today's world is fascinated with the middle brain.

We love stimulating, indulging, and feeding the monkey.

There are a number of problems with this enchantment.

The *Monkey brain* is addictive.

The *Monkey brain*, operating alone, is usually foolish.

Nature does not reward a reliance on folly.

Brain movement is not the same thing as brain utilization.

"The self-indulgent man craves for all pleasant things... and is led by his appetite to choose these at the cost of everything else." — Aristotle

Our head gets our attention by talking to us.

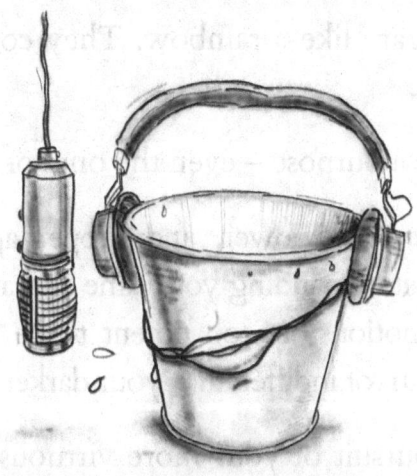

When it talks too much, it wears us out.

There are common signs our head is talking too much.

- Negativity
- Obsessions
- Memory loss
- Disturbed sleep
- Trouble listening
- Difficulty relaxing

All these things track back to that spoiled brain thing.

The brain is like a car motor.

It is designed to be off, idling, slow, or fast as needed.

A brain that races all the time is doomed to wreck.

"There is no thought, growth, or safety in an echo…thinking too little about things or thinking too much both make us obstinate and fanatical." — Pascal

The Heart

Human emotions are like a rainbow. They contain many colors and combinations.

All emotions have a purpose – even the ones of a darker nature.

Learning the potentials, power, and proper application of your emotions is a skillset demanding your time and attention from birth to death. Your emotions are too potent to be left to chance and impulse. In a vacuum of indifference, your darker feelings win.

The intentional pursuit of your more virtuous emotional nature is no easy enterprise. You will constantly face challenges and temptations that can capture you within your own darker spirit.

A compass toward your better nature is defined more surely by one thing than any other. It will require effort. It takes more energy to produce light than dark.

We do better to manage our emotions than condemn them.

Human emotions are neither good nor bad, right nor wrong.

It is how we turn them into action that sets that stage. We get to feel what we feel, but must control what we do.

- We can be angry without turning that anger loose.

- We can be hurt without collapsing into our pain.

- We can be fearful without surrendering.

In fact, that is the key to handling our emotional nature.

We are not blamable for what we feel – only for what we do.

"It's not much of a tail, but I'm sort of attached to it."
— A.A. Milne in Winnie the Pooh

We have the power to indirectly impact our emotions.

There is a rarely mentioned secret path to this maturity.

If we change our behavior, our feelings will follow.

That is something special to think about.

When we act in better fashion, we naturally feel better.

It is not an overnight thing, but it is a very reliable thing.

There is power in learning we can thereby seize our destiny.

But this secret works with good or bad actions.

"Thinking has, many a time, made me sad, darling; but doing never did in all my life... My precept is, "Do something, my sister, do good if you can; but, at any rate, do something." — Elizabeth Gaskell

The call to rob, neglect, or abuse our bucket is relentless.

The pains and pressures in every life – every day – nudge us.

Emotions can warn us of our error.

There are messenger emotions that are especially helpful:

Anger | Depression | Shame | Anxiety

These feelings push us to not waste our gifts.

They come not by chemical accident, nor to punish us.

They come to awaken us to the need to find a better way.

"And now here is my secret, a very simple secret: It is only with the heart that one can see rightly; what is essential is invisible to the eye."
— Antoine de Saint-Exupéry

Depression and anxiety are two very persuasive emotions.

Though painful, it helps to remember they come to teach us.

Knocking out the messenger is not a good idea.

We do that with addictions, prescriptions, distractions, etc.

Imagine giving painkillers to a cancer patient as a false cure.

Besides, knocked out messengers soon wake up.

And then they hit back even harder.

They only go away when we learn, engage, and change.

"There are all kinds of addicts, I guess. We all have pain. And we all look for ways to make the pain go away." — Sherman Alexie

Depression is the most common negative teaching emotion.

It is somewhat like a bad emotional soup.

When we indulge depression, we can quickly fill our bowl.

Blended and bottled up, it becomes grayish, brownish yuck.

That is a good description of what depression feels like.

Some depression on occasion is normal; a lot is not.

Depression can be like a wart that grows until we take action.

Depression is a call for growth, not surrender to despair.

"Mental pain is less dramatic than physical pain, but it is more common and also more hard to bear. The frequent attempt to conceal mental pain increases the burden: it is easier to say "My tooth is aching" than to say "My heart is broken." — C.S. Lewis

Anxiety can be the most painful human emotion of all.

It is intense. It is confusing.

It is hard to explain.

It makes us feel inadequate.

One might call anxiety the *highway to hell*.

A highway with three lanes – *fear, worry and self-rejection*.

Traveling those roads assures misery, getting lost, or a crash.

Taking good detours around will help us beat anxiety.

Anxiety is not an enemy – it flags a risky road.

"Your fear is 100% dependent on you for its survival."
— Steve Maraboli

Love is the greatest of emotions.

That is because it can fix things some emotions break.

Love is:

The great healer.

The great teacher.

The great uplifter.

The great comforter.

The great problem solver.

Though love is a powerful feeling, it finds its place in action.

And for most, love blooms most surely with repetition.

Anyone can learn to love, and everyone should.

"I'm selfish, impatient and a little insecure. I make mistakes, I am out of control and at times hard to handle. But if you can't handle me at my worst, then you sure as hell don't deserve me at my best."
— Marilyn Monroe

Anger destroys the bucket that holds it.

That is because anger is an ineffective *shield*.

That is because anger is *habit-forming*.

That is because anger is *catching*.

That is because anger is *toxic*.

Fortunately, forgiveness reigns as the great antidote.

When we forgive others, we are the primary beneficiary.

Sometimes we are even the one we have to forgive.

Ironically, forgiveness makes us stronger, not weaker.

No matter who, when, or for what, forgiveness is smart.

"*Anger ... it's a paralyzing emotion ... you can't get anything done. People sort of think it's an interesting, passionate, and igniting feeling — I don't think it's any of that — it's helpless ... it's absence of control — and I need all of my skills, all of the control, all of my powers ... and anger doesn't provide any of that — I have no use for it whatsoever.*" – Toni Morrison

Fear is like a python that can squeeze us to death.

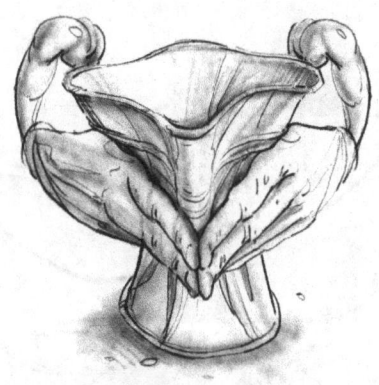

Liberating our head, heart, hand & spirit does the opposite.

We all have a fear button – everyone.

And one of the most common fears is a fear of people.

That is usually because we have been harmed by people.

So many of the good things of life center on people.

Love, support, and intimacy encourage us to keep trying.

Practiced courage is the counter to fear of *anything*.

"*I must not fear. Fear is the mind-killer. Fear is the little-death that brings total obliteration. I will face my fear. I will permit it to pass over me and through me. And when it has gone past, I will turn the inner eye to see its path. Where the fear has gone there will be nothing. Only I will remain.*" — Frank Herbert

Some emotions make us feel powerful – others the opposite.

That sets us up for a dilemma.

Should we feel what we feel, or swap our emotions?

If anger feels stronger than fear, then why not chose anger?

If arrogance seems better than doubt, why not go there?

Running from real emotions causes emotional build up.

It also makes us foolish, reactive, and fake.

Responding with our true feelings grounds us in maturity.

It takes the greater strength to feel what we feel and be real.

"The truth might hurt, but it is never your enemy."
— Craig Lounsbrough

In a big world, everyone sometimes feels small and flawed.

These dark emotions can trigger more darkness.

"I am not very good."

"The world is not very good."

"Then how can life be very good?"

Feelings of inadequacy can also lead to destructive choices.

That creates a vicious cycle that generates more misery.

There will be bad moments, bad things, and bad people.

There will be good moments, good things, and good people.

It will be up to us to decide which captures our enthusiasm.

"We're going to have to let truth scream louder to our souls than the lies that have infected us." — Beth Moore

Your heart is designed like a shock-absorber on a car.

It cushions the potholes on life's highway.

But we still need to absorb our share of the bumps.

There are times we simply need to be still and just feel.

Our heart sorts emotions – a babbling brain worsens them.

Think of a garbage disposal.

The head is prone to clumsy attempts to discard our feelings.

Our heart simply grinds them up so we can move forward.

"Insecurity, inferiority complex, past failures, and comparison are not your friend. Don't allow them to grow roots. The world is waiting for everything you've got to bring to the table." — Andrena Sawyer

We do not get to choose what we feel.

We should *always* choose what we do with what we feel.

Feeling fearful does not mean we have to cower.

Feeling angry does not mean we need to lash out.

We can feel one way and act another, and still be genuine.

Emotions are more like a ship's sail than a ship's rudder.

Our feelings should help fuel versus determine our course.

"One's dignity may be assaulted, vandalized and cruelly mocked, but it can never be taken away unless it is surrendered." — Michael J. Fox

The Hand

The part of you that actually does things is often taken for granted. Yet it is the hand of action that gives impact to the brain, opportunity to the heart, and truth to the spirit.

How you apply your hand to the world is, in fact, the ultimate determinant of your life course. Your behavior is also the most important measuring instrument of your character, ability, and commitments.

There is a simple reason that your hand contains so much power. Controlling your head is never easy.

You have little or no control over what you feel, and the word control doesn't even enter the script when it comes to your spirit. It is only in your actions that you can find the power of solid self-regulation.

Thus, you are sized up most fairly by how you apply your hand to your head, heart, and spirit to life than any other gauge of merit.

It is not fair to judge you by that over which you have no control. Neither is it just to fail to measure you by that over which you do have control.

We all have a place in the world – *every* single one of us.

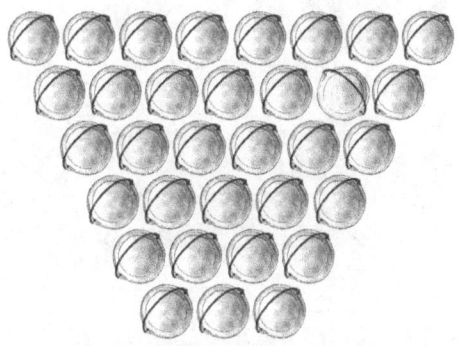

For some rare people, their place comes *naturally*.

Others are fortunate to search and *find* their place.

But for most of us, it is not that easy.

We have to *build* our place in the world.

And there is a catch.

Most of us have to build ourselves at the same time.

"What if I fall – oh but my darling, what if you fly?"
—J. M. Barrie, Peter Pan

The body also tells us we cannot abuse our *soft spots*.

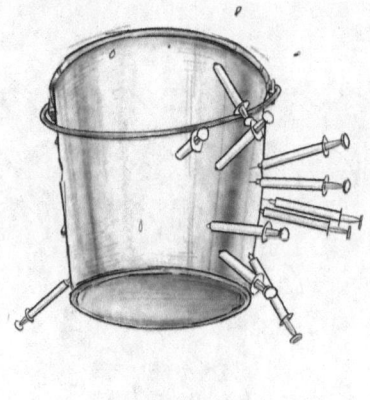

It does that in million ways, but drugs offer one example.

No drug – *legal or not* – exists without side effects.

No drug works on one thing without impacting others.

Drugs can help us deal with the consequences of bad choices.

But the majority of drugs treat symptoms versus causes.

That impact counts and can be helpful.

But it is better to take care of what we have to begin with.

"Drugs take you to hell, disguised as heaven." — Donald Lyn Frost

There is a difference in living a life of quality and quantity.

Much of the latter occurs through *distraction therapy*.

Distraction therapy has us confusing *doing* with *living*.

Achievements, successes, and bucket lists are fine.

But at the end of life, those things will lose their luster.

How we love, learn, labor, live and listen will be our mark.

Trophies for putting our hand to the world are a nice thing.

Tasting life at a deeper level lays a footing for a better thing.

"You will never reach your destination if you stop and throw stones at every dog that barks." — Winston S. Churchill

We live on a self-correcting planet.

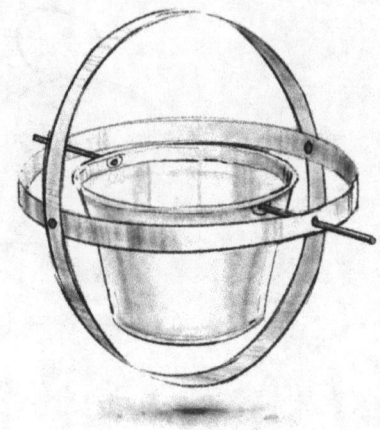

It is constantly readjusting itself, sometimes unpleasantly.

We operate off that same self-correcting system.

Extremes in our behavior lead to consequence.

If we keep our balance, we can avoid a lot of pain.

But that balance requires we restrain appetites and actions.

Humans prefer independence over limits and accountability.

Self-corrections arrive not to punish, but to realign.

"Nobody ever did, or ever will, escape the consequences of his choices."
– Alfred A. Montaper

The Spirit

There is something inside you around you, and beyond you that cannot be detected with the aid of taste, sound, touch, sight, or smell. It is an influence not readily discerned by the everyday reaches of human experience.

The existence of a unifying force in the universe is both controversial and crucial. We struggle to accept it or to do without it.

There is a reason mankind has never stopped searching for something bigger, better, and wiser. Though you are profoundly powerful in your ability to lay your head, heart, and hand to the world, too often that combination falls short in its impact and ability to satisfy and justify existence.

The search for a higher power – like most things in life – rests most responsibly in your own hands. You have to be personally invested in the pursuit, for spiritual clarity does not come cheaply. At best, you can only glimpse the possibilities through the example, assertions, and teachings of others.

Those who unbendingly declare "there is no God" or "God is undeniable" take equal liberties with sensibility. Truth finds no sanctuary amidst the endless mazes of the willful mind or the narrow comforts of dogma.

It is possible to hold tightly to a personal spiritual belief system, yet carry no matching wish to force that view upon others. Spiritual sincerity is birthed in the volunteer, not the abducted.

Still, it would be a mistake to suggest that your spiritual journey is a casual consideration. In fact, just the opposite is true. For it is in the spiritual that you will find the glue which binds your other parts.

For the present you remain free to choose any spiritual path that you wish. Hopefully that choice will be grounded in astuteness and a deeper eye.

It is helpful that America's existence and cultural structure is grounded in the Christian faith.

With that foundation in mind, there is guidance to be found in the Biblical reference of Luke 17:20-21

— And when he was demanded of the Pharisees, when the kingdom of God should come, he answered them and said, "The kingdom of God cometh not with observation. Neither shall they say, Lo here! or, lo there! for, behold, the kingdom of God is within you."

Regardless of the spiritual path you choose to take, this scriptural statement holds direct application.

There is no mine more difficult to work than the one that is within you...

History reveals a persisting truism.

There is more to us than our head, heart, and hand.

We are bigger than just a collection of parts.

Inside us all resides something greater, more powerful.

It is a force of spirit uniquely dedicated to that which is good.

It stands in firm competition to that which is not good.

We live in a challenging world.

This force within us is an essential source of support.

"Science is not only compatible with spirituality; it is a profound source of spirituality." — Carl Sagan

There are an endless number of man-made religions.

With differing messages, finding a spiritual compass is hard.
If we listen, it is possible to hear an inner voice of aid.
It tells us that thinking, feeling, and doing is not enough.
It tells us that life needs something more – something else...

• *A belief in where we came from.*

• *A belief in what we should be doing while we are here.*

• *A belief in where we are going when we leave here.*

• *A belief that there is something more than just us.*

To ignore this aspect of our life is a great error.

"We are not human beings having a spiritual experience. We are spiritual beings having a human experience."
— Pierre Teilhard de Chardin

Not everyone believes in having a spiritual anchor.

But those seeking authentic spirituality need not look far.

Consider the inner voice that warns of wrongs *before* we act.

Note the *visions* of those who have faced death and returned.

Then there are the earthly *intricacies* mocking the big bang.

Consider the stunning *complexities* of our DNA.

And that our universe mirrors that same complexity.

Reason can begin, but never secure our spiritual connection.

"My intellect is a wonderful thing and it is helpful, but I now see that there is another, deeper place of intelligence within me—and everyone else. Once we tap into it, we can begin to transform our lives."
— Ankush Jain

A leap of faith is required for both the Big Bang *or* a big God.

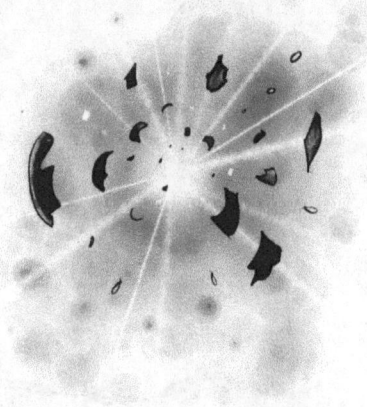

There are arguments either way, and no one knows for sure.

Science uses logic, but that logic has gaping holes.

Spiritualty offers assurance, but that can evolve into dogma.

We all have to make our own choices.

Does our here and hereafter rest on an accident, or a plan?

We can make a religion out of almost any belief.

But does that belief uplift us or just bang us around?

> *The conscious attempt to be a good person without Christ is as legalistic as an attempt to make it into Heaven through empty religiosity."* — Criss Jam

It is possible to test the strength of a spiritual value system

The Bible describes a spiritual person as a truth seeker.

Arrogance, comfort, and anger rarely partner with truth.

Faith from fear, worry, and self-criticism is equally suspect.

None of those things are supported in the Bible.

Religion, like all things of man, is prone to manipulation.

There is a way to find a point of spiritual truth.

Spiritual sincerity is *never* a path to evil.

"When we give up on what draws us near to God, we become like beasts." — L. Michael Morales

One can isolate the spiritually real from the fake.

Almost all religions and humanistic beliefs talk about *love*.

Since all people need love, that focus is a compelling draw.

One can part the wheat from the chaff with another word.

Spiritual sincerity is also grounded in *responsibility*.

Any screenplay selling love without responsibility is a scam.

A true compass must reliably point in the right direction.

"My religion consists of a humble admiration of the illimitable superior spirit who reveals himself in the slight details we are able to perceive with our frail and feeble mind." — Albert Einstein

Spiritual choice comes down to a few special decisions.

When we look at the things of the world, are we heartened?

When we look toward spiritual values, are we strengthened?

Which course best demonstrates reliability?

It is not possible to jointly follow the things of man and faith.

It is true that the spirit is neither visible nor tangible.

But have we found *anything* of man that can truly replace it?

"I had rather mistrust my own capacity than God's justice."
— Alexis de Tocqueville

One thing is certain, we live in battle between good and evil.

But we can find the line between goodness and darkness.

Remember that good is usually hard, and evil is usually easy.

Each of us also has a go-between inside us that knows.

To benefit, we have to listen to that messenger.

Faith helps us in the walk toward the light.

Overlooking our spirit sends us stumbling back into the dark.

"The demon is a liar. He will lie to confuse us; but he will also mix lies with the truth to attack us. His attack is psychological, Damien. And powerful."— William Peter Blatty, The Exorcist

Chapter Eleven
Soft Wisdom

Stealing or exploiting your *soft spots* is an effortless undertaking. And you can complete this unwitting task faster than you may imagine.

Witness those addicted to methamphetamine. Theirs is a drug that takes the head, heart, and hand to extraordinary heights of intensity. It feels good to do that.

But the price for this artificial pursuit is higher than the high. Meth fools you into believing that it is the drug that takes you up and away from the harsh realities of life. In truth, the power for that escape comes from within. Your own *soft spots* fuel the rocket.

Over time – and not really much time – meth addiction can rob your *soft spots* with remarkable efficiency. For with every moment of high comes a matching moment of low. More surely than slowly, you will consume yourself from within.

Every escape from real life has a charge. The greater the escape, the greater the price.

Unfortunately, the surface prices like loss of a job, loss of a spouse, loss of health, and other visible injuries are nothing in comparison to the hidden losses of your tiny, vulnerable spots of energy, life, and light.

Like in all hard things, there is opportunity hidden in this mix. It is possible to repair and renew a measure of your *soft spots*.

Though it is extremely easy to deplete your supply, it is anything but easy to reverse the harms you or others can do to you.

But it is possible. Here is a short course on how.

- Who Runs Who -

He learned the power of exercise early in life.

That gift came mostly from a rough-around-the-edges coach named Jim Levine. Though hard on the outside, he had a big heart that could not help but encourage even the skinny, apprehensive and talentless.

His coach's touch in unsuccessful ventures in track and football stuck harder than he imagined amidst the travails of both. After school, in basic training, he was the second fastest of fifty men. He marveled at where that ability came from, but he knew a big part of it came from Jim Levine.

That sweet gentleman's soft spot admonition to "pick 'em up and lay 'em down" echoes even as he runs today. Thank you, sir, for that gift.

He finally learned to master his head thanks to running. He and Pepper had a track through downtown that served them through many years.

To practice getting control of his constantly running brain, he would reset his head every city block or so. The mission was simply to stop thinking for that block and then reset at the next block. Sometimes he would struggle to not think.

Sometimes he would repeat the word "no" or "stop" every time a thought popped up and tried to take over. His favorite approach was to simply let the thought come, but tell himself to "lay 'em down" as it did so. Thanks, again, coach.

Running six days a week gave him lots of practice opportunities.

Like the run itself, he gradually conditioned his brain to the idea that he was in charge of it versus it being in charge of him. Knowing that managing one's own thoughts is one of the toughest life skills to master, he enjoyed the accomplishment.

It did not come easily. Sometimes he had to get a little aggressive with the thoughts. That anger was not at himself or his brain, but at all those relentless little pieces of mental activity – good and bad – that competed to control his mind.

Of all the self-management things he ever learned to do – mastering his anger, his critical inner voice, the importance of being a force of love, and controlling his thoughts – the last one was the toughest one by far.

It took him half a lifetime to understand that learning this skill was supremely important. Much of the rest to figure out a way to pull it off.

He would not let himself write this book until he could...

Bad conflict is the No. 1 source of broken relationships.

Relationships are important, and so is conflict management.

Fuss we will, but there are helpful and harmful ways to do so.

Right-wrong, good-bad, and win-lose struggles do not work.

Yes, it is true that conflict is not always within our control.

How we personally participate in conflict very much is.

Resisting anger and facing issues vs. attacking people helps.

It also helps to learn that when we both win – we both win.

"In dwelling, live close to the ground. In thinking, keep to the simple. In conflict, be fair and generous. In governing, don't try to control. In work, do what you enjoy. In family life, be completely present." — Lao Tzu

We are each born in a unique and accessible greenhouse.

Parents, siblings, teachers, friends, and others can enter.

What they do while they are there can have a big impact.

In adolescence, things change.

The door and windows to our greenhouse begin to close.

From that point, our self-esteem rests chiefly in our hands.

We are not told of this shift in accountability.

We must build on the self we have and fix what was broken.

"Don't you dare take the lazy way. It's too easy to excuse yourself because of your ancestry. Don't let me catch you doing it! Now - look close at me so you will remember. Whatever you do, it will be you who do." — John Steinbeck, East of Eden

We live in a hyper-sexualized world.

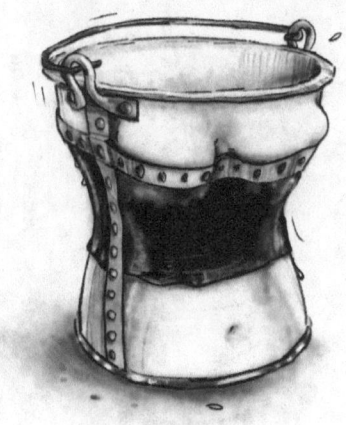

But sex is a two-edged sword that can take us to bad places.

One stimulation for our fascination with sex is addiction.

Sex has a drug-like impact that compels us.

We can easily get addicted to the high and lose judgment.

It is easy for our sexuality to thereby become corrupted.

Sex tracks to hormones, conditioning, lust, fantasy, and love.

The last one is the only one that lasts.

"There is no dignity when the human dimension is eliminated from the person. In short, the problem with pornography is not that it shows too much of the person, but that it shows far too little."
— Pope John Paul II

Humans are complex mechanisms.

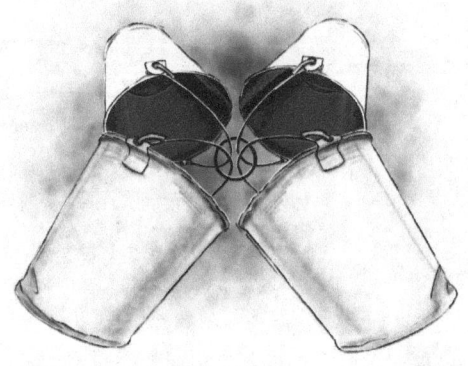

All our parts interact with the potential to hurt or aid others.

Consider the following:

The head is the source of *intelligence*.

The head and the heart are the source of *wisdom*.

The head, heart, and hand are the source of *understanding*.

The head, heart, hand, and spirit are the source of *enlightenment*.

It is easy to see that neglecting one part impacts others.

Learning to pull the power of our parts together is a skill.

And it is a skill we should pursue for a lifetime.

"If you're not confused, you're not paying attention." — Tom Peters

Nurturing new life into adulthood is a special responsibility.

There are lots of means to fulfilling this responsibility. But the biggest key is unsurprisingly found in the word *love*. That love must be given without conditions, and in all forms.

- Values
- Affection
- Attention
- Discipline
- Protection
- Boundaries
- Role models
- Nourishment
- Encouragement
- Opportunities for success

There is no substitute for love as a childrearing necessity and intact families are a matchless vessel for nurturing that love.

"The greater a child's terror, and the earlier it is experienced, the harder it becomes to develop a strong and healthy sense of self."
— Nathaniel Branden

People are meant to be moveable objects.

That is why stagnancy is so toxic.

Everything about us is designed to be in motion.

That includes our head, heart, hand and spirit.

When our parts sit too long, we rust, shrink, and decay.

Our *soft spots* follow that lead.

"Happiness is a state of activity." — Aristotle

Addiction is the real No. 1 health crisis in America.

It is not just drugs and alcohol that are fueling this calamity.

We can get addicted to just about anything.

We cannot get addicted to anything without consequences.

Without consequences, we would all be addicts.

Even with consequence, addiction is a relentless slayer.

"I have absolutely no pleasure in the stimulants in which I sometimes so madly indulge. It has not been in the pursuit of pleasure that I have periled life and reputation and reason. It has been the desperate attempt to escape from torturing memories, from a sense of insupportable loneliness and a dread of some strange impending doom."
— Edgar Allan Poe

Stress, a form of pressure, is a relentless reality of life.

With care we can learn to handle stress.

There are two kinds of stress – one is painful – one is deadly.

Linear stress has a beginning, a middle, and an end.

The second – circular – finds us stuck in an endless hoop.

That coil can wear us down in the mire of despair.

Be not deceived by despair.

There is always a way to turn a circle into a line.

"I must lose myself in action, lest I wither in despair."
– Alfred Lord Tennyson

Relentless stress takes no mercy on any part of who we are.

Unaddressed, it can percolate within us.

Most people have one or more stress-vulnerable body parts.

Some include headaches, gastro distress, and joint pain.

A stress-battered immune system can also get our attention.

Recurring physical ailments often reveal harmful pressures.

When we listen, we can see the need to find a better way.

"As her analyst had told her: the deeper buried the distress, the further into the body it went. The digestive system was about as far as it could go to hide." — Richard Matheson

There is a difference in the impact of a conscience and guilt.

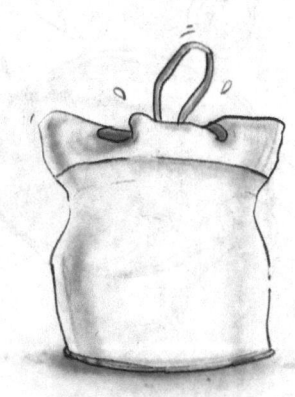

Guilt is designed to warn us, but it can be used to punish us.

Conscience warns us too, but usually calls for positive action.

Transient guilt can raise awareness, but lurking guilt is toxic.

Conscience, on the other hand, lingers to point us to good.

People throwing guilt about helter-skelter are manipulators.

A person of good conscience uplifts and quietly encourages.

"*Chronic remorse, as all the moralists are agreed, is a most undesirable sentiment. If you have behaved badly, repent, make what amends you can and address yourself to the task of behaving better next time. On no account brood over your wrongdoing. Rolling in the muck is not the best way of getting clean.*" — Aldous Huxley

Few hurts penetrate as deeply as the loss of a loved one.

The resulting grief leaves a hole in our heart *and* life.

The abrupt, stark permanence of death makes it so.

But there is a difference in the type of hole our grief creates.

There are holes made of resentment, despair, and resistance.

Then there are holes made of sorrow, pain, and mourning.

The first generate a void that struggles to heal.

The latter creates an emotional wound that mends with time.

How would our loved one want us to face our loss?

"Only people who are capable of loving strongly can also suffer great sorrow, but this same necessity of loving serves to counteract their grief and heals them." — Leo Tolstoy

Everything on planet earth can be turned to good or bad.

A priest can be a bridge to God or molest for lust.

A physician can heal or exploit for money.

A politician can lead or manipulate for power.

A parent can love toward growth or abuse toward misery.

Everything can be taken to a good or bad place.

Rejecting things because they have been misused is an error.

Reject the abuser, not the opportunity they abused.

We do not quit eating bread because we meet a moldy slice.

"It takes very little to govern good people. Very little. And bad people can't be governed at all. Or if they could, I never heard of it."
— Cormac McCarthy

We have become a society of patches.

We fix so little, but temporarily band-aide so much.

Why? Because it is just easier.

It easier to enable an addict than to hold them to recovery.

It is easier to coddle a criminal than to fairly apply justice.

It is easier to take a pill than to alter a harmful lifestyle.

It is easier to gloss over decline than to care for or guide.

The things of man come easier than the things of God.

But patches unfailingly hold a fatal flaw.

They soon yield, unravel, and reveal our holes.

"Like most shortcuts, it was an ill-chosen route"
— Washington Irving, The Devil and Tom Walker

Technology drains us like it drains our phone battery.

It does that in many, many ways

It does that with addictive apps.

It does that with a constant parade of negative news.

It does that with light waves that activate the brain.

It does that with drama and chaos.

It does that with manipulative algorithms.

Technology is fine, but like all good things, it has limits.

Too much tech will drain your brain and kidnap the rest.

"Technology is degeneration of native intelligence and promotion of Artificial Intelligence. In short - Destruction!" — PB Flower

Insecure people use control as a compensation.

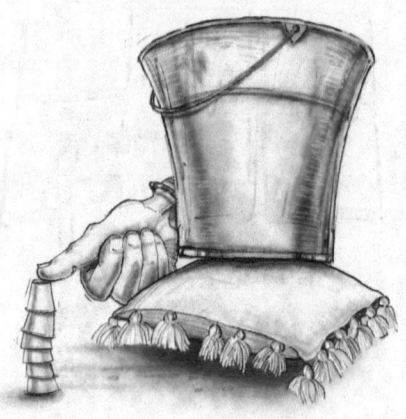

We can't find peace in our own life, so we try to run others.

It seldom works out well, so we try harder.

That takes us to anger, negativity, denial, and violence.

Witness the malice of political dictators addicted to control.

A happy life requires that we run ourselves, not others.

That is more than enough to keep most of us busy.

"Be not angry that you cannot make others as you wish them to be, since you cannot make yourself as you wish to be."
— Thomas à Kempis, The Imitation of Christ

Many recognize that there is a national mental health crisis.

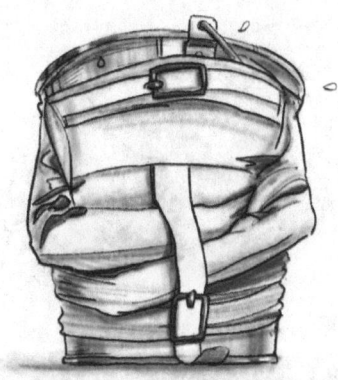

There is fact in this opinion, but there is also a deeper truth.

There is a difference in a maturity and mental health crisis.

We are going through a time where immaturity is in vogue.

It is fun to unleash one's inner demons.

But that does not mean it is healthy or without consequence.

There is a big problem with this form of self-indulgence.

Immaturity does not stand alone – it seeks company.

Immaturity hides in the foundation of most mental illness.

"You have attained maturity; display it for us, if you please."
— Mary Janice Davidson, Swimming Without a Net

We all need love, and there are many places to find it.

Some of us have a strong belief in God's love.

Then there is importance of learning to love ourselves.

Often overlooked is the power that giving love holds.

Love from others is the form of love we prize the most.

Ironically, we can fill most of our needs from the first three.

We are in charge of embracing those forms of love.

The last is in the hands of others, and is the least reliable.

"When you show others love, you are shown love. When you give love, you receive love." — Donald L. Hicks

Human beings are social creatures.

Because we are people, we need other people. There are 3 ways to define good relationships:

- *Both* work to grow self and one another.

- *Both* work to handle conflict in a good way.

- *Both* prioritize commitment, truth, and contribution.

That is it.

But that is plenty.

We not only need people; we need them in the right way.

"Sometimes you give more love, sometimes you need more love. Be with the person you can balance with." — Elizabeth Bourgeret

There are many things over which we have no direct control.

We cannot control our *childhood, color,* or *culture.*

We are in charge of our *character, choices,* and *convictions.*

All these things matter, but we face a relentless truism.

It is what we control that most defines our future.

Character, choices, and convictions rest firmly in our hands.

"Incredible change happens in your life when you decide to take control of what you do have power over instead of craving control over what you don't." — Steve Maraboli

Mistakes are part and parcel to the human experience.

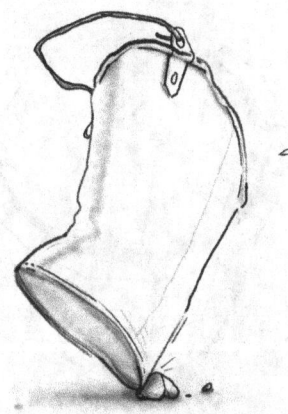

Everyone makes them, and it is okay - with a few conditions.

Coping with mistakes is a four-step process.

Letting others pile on our errors is *not* one of those steps.

Step One is to own our mistakes – *accountably*.

Step Two is to learn from our mistakes – *intentionally*.

Step Three is to forgive our mistakes – *unconditionally*.

Step four is to lay down our mistakes – *permanently*.

Each step lays the foundation for the next step.

Thus, we cannot skip steps if we are to press on.

"We learn from failure, not from success!" — Bram Stoker, Dracula

From those to whom much is given – much is expected.

Nature uses this formula to keep us honest.

Gaps between our ability and our lifestyle generate misery.

The bigger the gap, the greater our unhappiness.

The solutions?

• Make use of what we have.

• Grow what we have.

• Celebrate what we have!

And we all have more than we know.

"Reflect upon your present blessings -- of which every man has many -- not on your past misfortunes, of which all men have some."
— Charles Dickens

Replenishing our *soft spots* is not a fast process.

It's sort of like filling a bathtub – one drip at a time.

That is why we live in a world so dedicated to *hard spots*.

It is always easier to steal than to build.

In this case, we steal mostly from ourselves.

Doing so is like committing a robbery on our own home.

"All happiness depends on courage and work." — Honoré de Balzac

We live in a world of infinite possibilities.

We are breathlessly fortunate.

But we have to take risks with those blessings.

When moving forward, we are faced with three options:

- We can do what pleases others.

- We can do what pleases us.

- We can do what is right.

Sometimes, we can do one thing and accomplish all three.

But if forced to make one choice, always pick the last one.

"Doing the right thing even when no one is looking is easy if I remember that I am not in this life alone and that my task is to please God...not people." — Sandra C. Bibb

People-Care is an important part of being human.

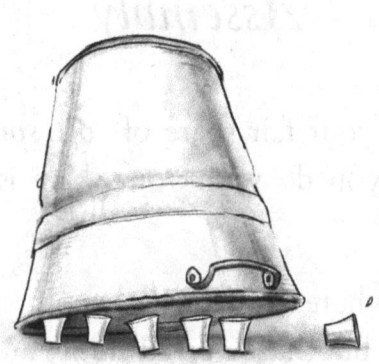

All people benefit from proper care – especially self-care.

And we will all have times when we need other people's care.

People-Care comes in many forms:

Love, validation, opportunity, support, encouragement, models, reward, freedom, skills, gratitude, examples, protection, and appreciation are all examples of people maintenance tools.

People who are properly cared for become better people.

It is a responsibility best not left to chance or impulse.

Better people make for a better and softer world.

"Taking care of others, helping others, ultimately is the way to discover your own joy and to have a happy life." – Archbishop Desmond Tutu

Chapter Twelve

Assembly

You are born with your fair share of *soft spots*. What you and the people around you do with your share is where things get tricky.

Fairytale endings where true love, happiness, and success are found are attractive, but those opportunities are rare.

For most, your landing spot in the world will not be given or discovered, it will be built.

That is what life is most surely about – taking your gifts and talents and facing the challenges you encounter as you reach for your potentials.

You were not put here to be happy ever after. As wonderful as that sounds, it would surely become boring.

Happy is important, but so too are growth, opportunity, challenge, and adventure.

But you have to be willing to risk yourself, aim yourself, and work yourself...

- Pain is a Propellant -

It took him time – a lot of time – to figure out that pain was like gasoline. When properly used, it was less likely to stop him than push him.

Pain felt like duct tape. It wrapped itself around you like a python attempting to choke the life out of everything that was worthy and hopeful. It was sticky, icky, and picky. It was like being set on fire where there was no water.

But ultimately, he learned that none of these things were true.

Pain was necessary, even crucial, to some of the most important things in life. Things like growth, love, achievement, wisdom, and generosity.

Were it not for the painful inadequacy he felt in most of his childhood, he would not have reached so high or crammed so much into the years after he left home.

Were it not for the pains of earlier relationships, his ability to love and be loved would never have been honed to his fuller potentials. Through his pain, he gradually figured out that, with rare exception, love was an earned skill more often than a natural talent.

Were it not for the pains of war, and school, and work, he would not have felt the need to push himself to better levels and higher potentials. The tremendous energy necessary to stretching himself was never found in places of comfort.

Were it not for the pain of feeling that he knew too little about too much and that he was an imposter of competency, he would not have craved wisdom. The hurt he so often experienced per a deficit of knowledge prompted a search for understanding that would help him fill the void and evade future stumbles.

Were it not for the pain of deprivation, he would not have understood the blessings of bounty and living in a world with so many opportunities to give of ourselves and thereby – ever so importantly – turn out of ourselves.

Gasoline had to be contained, handled with care, and applied correctly – as it is with everything else of life that is coupled to goodness and high value.

Similarly, his pain had to be managed, faced, and channelled. That required one to resist the temptations of addressing pain through escape, avoidance, and denial.

Pain and gasoline were equally potent and filled with potential.

So was he. So are we all...

Fear is an emotion that can rarely be fixed with thinking.

At best, thinking will provide only temporary distraction.

At worst, it will aggravate and expand our fear.

Fear is like the unpleasantries of poison ivy.

The more you scratch it, the more it will itch and spread.

There is only one sure source of relief from fear — action.

Out of action comes potential success, and success kills fear.

Listen to a fearful heart, but never put it in control.

A leap of courage will conquer a heap of fear.

"Your emotions make you human. Even the unpleasant ones have a purpose. Don't lock them away. If you ignore them, they just get louder and angrier." — Sabaa Tahir

Men and women have differing *soft spots*.

Women have a closer union to three things:
- Caring
- Civilizing
- Connecting

Men have a closer union to three different things:
- Producing
- Providing
- Protecting

Our similarities and uniqueness are equally important.

We complement one another.

That symmetry should be nurtured and celebrated.

"The rest of us have never embraced your victim mentality; we are not victims. We are people, the same way that men are. We are equal, yet different. We, unlike you, realize that is not mutually exclusive."
— Lori Ziganto

Potty-training is a necessary milestone in childhood.

Managing one's behind and bladder are important life skills.

Why is it that no one teaches us how to control our brain?

The behind and the bladder leave messes we can see.

The brain creates even bigger messes we cannot see.

As adults, most of us have to potty-train our own brain.

It is much harder than potty-training those first two parts.

"If someone in the street were entrusted with your body, you would be furious. Yet you entrust your mind to anyone around who happens to insult you, and allow it to be troubled and confused. Aren't you ashamed of that?" — Epictetus

We should strive to stand for something.

That means that in a harsh world, we must stand up.

Courtesy is an option — passivity, not so much.

Our *soft spots* need protection from abuse, theft, and attack. It is important that we find a healthy style for standing up.

Courage and conviction work better than anger and malice.

It is easy to be nasty and mean — hard to be strong but nice.

Light is soft, but it consumes darkness with fierce efficiency.

"Be sure you put your feet in the right place, and then stand firm.
– Abraham Lincoln

Making our way through life requires skill.

Those skills can be negative or positive – it is our choice.

Malice, selfishness, anger, and violence are negative skills.

Love, charity, forgiveness, and hard work are positive skills.

Being a thief requires skill as surely as being a policeman.

But the outcome is very different.

Life events may push us toward good or bad skills.

But we have the amazing sway of choice on which we absorb.

"Destiny is not a matter of chance; it is a matter of choice. It is not a thing to be waited for, it is a thing to be achieved."
— William Jennings Bryan

Everyone needs help sometimes.

There are two kinds of help:
- The kind of help that helps us get by.
- The kind of help that helps us get ahead.

The first makes us smaller. The second is a necessity.

The best help comes in the form of example, encouragement, love, and support that builds the person being helped.

Help that enables a person to avoid their accountabilities is not really help at all and is often designed more to advance the interests of the helper than those being helped.

Helping others in the right way helps the helper too.

Enabling and loving are thus very much *not* the same thing.

"Allowing others to suffer the consequences of their own actions, without enabling them, is the best motivation for them to undertake the difficult task of change." — Darlene Lancer

Sometimes our *soft spots* need rest.

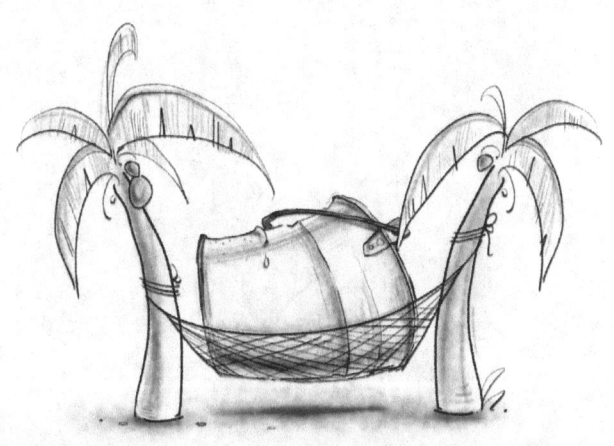

Feeling unpleasant emotions, or ups and downs, is normal.

Without the downs, we would not see the blessings of ups.

We must also experience times of neutrality or flatness.

Though peddling is important, coasting helps us recover.

The only way to feel good all the time is to rob our bucket.

Too much time spent riding or coasting can lead to crashing.

Life is a long trip, and empty buckets do not make it.

"Proud of the work I've done and savoring the hours of rest I've earned." — Ronda Rousey

Life is rarely easy, and difficulties are part of the recipe.

There is a simple way to find our best response.

Think of a road – on either side of that road is a deep ditch.

Every problem similarly finds us with extreme solutions.

For example, we can run from a snake or try to kill it.

We can also just stand still and let it slide away.

The road to reason always stands between the ditches.

"One of the secrets of successful living is found in the word balance, referring to the avoidance of harmful extremes. We need food, but we should not overeat. We should work, but not make work our only activity. We should play, but not let play rule us. Throughout life, it will be important to find the safety of the middle ground rather than the imbalance of the extremes." — James C. Dobson

Chapter Thirteen
Leftovers

There are a few tidbits that do not fit neatly into a particular box. That is okay, because the same box that can contain things can also keep them hidden.

What follows are a collection of stand-alone pages that may be of service. You live in turbulent times. These not-so-obvious people skills can help you stay ahead of the darkness.

We live in a time when an increasing number of smart people are stumbling over choices that are anything but smart.

This trend is starkly visible in the worlds of business, governance, national defense, medicine, education, science, religion, entertainment, economics and media. At times it seems that most if not all of our primary institutions of cultural integrity have, in lockstep, lost their integrity.

This pattern of social regression is as bewildering as it is alarming.

But there is comfort. Our society's massive indifference to our historical equation of success may be reaching its apex of absurdity. One can only test a cliff so long before there is a fall or, better for all of us, the dawning wisdom of recovery.

In the interim we still have ourselves. We will never lose the power of personal choice – and though that gift may be battered and bruised by external forces – it cannot be destroyed.

No matter how bad it gets around us, we will always be able to succeed within us.

– An Equation for Success –

At some point he began to understand that authentic wisdom is seldom a product of lofty thought or spontaneous bursts of enlightenment. Most useful knowledge seemed to be more often crafted in the crucibles of time, experience, study, and hard work.

And so it was with an insight that he crafted from parts that seemed to have no direct connection.

The first fragment centered on the importance of **_liberty_** as a central foundation for a positive life experience. He noted that too often mankind seems willing to exchange the clear value of freedom for the illusion of security.

The second part keyed on **_opportunity_**. Without opportunity to grow, achieve, and secure our place in the world, hope and happiness are illusive and fragile pursuits.

The third part – **_responsibility_** – was the toughest sell of all. He figured out that a society that exempts its membership from personal accountability is doomed to hardship.

His last word centered on **_prosperity_**. It was about so much more that wealth. Intricately woven into prosperity were comfort, trust, safety, and relief from material anguish.

At some point, he recognized that in unity, these four words represented a uniquely American success equation:

Liberty + Opportunity + Responsibility = Prosperity.

He understood that there were those who pretended that it is possible to cheat this formula, leave out pieces, and produce the same outcome. They were *always* very wrong.

Pursuing glorified sympathies is tempting. Success at any worthy mission also requires sincerity...

Teenagers face unique challenges.

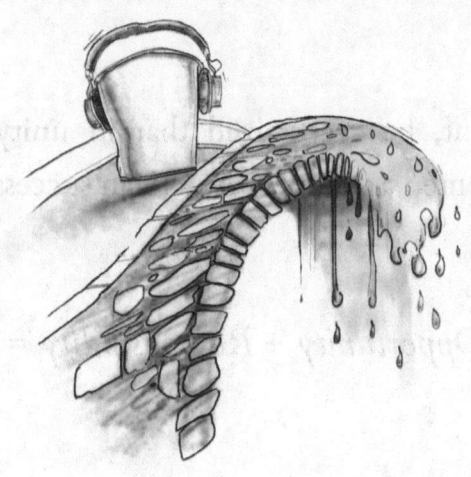

They travel on a high, icy, slippery, melting bridge.

We must all cross that bridge, or risk getting trapped.

To do so requires that we scramble, slip, slide, and strive.

Adolescence is not a time for time out.

Our bridge will not wait for us.

But climbing our bridge can be fun, exciting, and rewarding.

We cannot surrender to fear or idleness to avoid doing that.

Getting stuck on the wrong side of the bridge is a bad thing.

"If a society is to preserve stability and a degree of continuity, it must learn how to keep its adolescents from imposing their tastes, values, and fantasies on everyday life." — Eric Hoffer

There are many paths to building personal identity.

The most reflexive are resistance, herding, and anger.

These are easy, primitive, and rarely produce good outcomes.

There are better sources of identity that take work.

Laboring, loving, learning, and living right are good paths.

Sort of like a house of bricks is better than sticks or mud.

Better does not mean easy – it just means better.

"He allowed himself to be swayed by his conviction that human beings are not born once and for all on the day their mothers give birth to them, but that life obliges them over and over again to give birth to themselves."
— Gabriel García Márquez, Love in the Time of Cholera

Gender uncertainties are a sore subject.

There are many views on what is the right and wrong track. Unfortunate absurdities abound. Here are some samples:

Allowing children to make early determinations on their gender with the support of public-school officials, physicians, and parents is a form of abuse. There is a reason we do not let those under sixteen drive, drink, vote, buy a house, or decide whether to brush their teeth. Exempting gender choices is a bit like serving undercooked chicken for dinner. It is fraught with consequences.

Any movement that is characterized by anger, infighting, and antagonism to discussion and debate reveals the limits of its authenticity and maturity.

Just because people say things with enthusiasm and intensity, does not mean they are right, or that people with a softer approach are wrong. Truth does not require a hammer to drive in its point.

Identity confusion is normal in a confusing world.

Anything life-changing should be approached very carefully.

"Do you place your faith in words or the things you talk about but not in the truth and without a care for how you act?"
– John Bunyan, Pilgrim's Progress

Ever feel like your head is full of bees?

Two kinds like it there —red hornets and honey bees.

Hornets sting with harmful, harsh, and angry thoughts.

Honey bee thoughts are sweet, productive, and helpful.

It takes minutes for either to build a nest in our head.

Red hornet thoughts torment relentlessly.

They need to be swatted down immediately.

Before their nest crowds out our honey bee thoughts.

"When we allow negative messages to fester in our head, they take on a life of their own." — Lolly Daskal

It is a myth we can think about many things at a time.

What we actually do is a quick switch back and forth.

That means one thought can intercept another thought.

And that a bad thought can be replaced with a good one.

That is something we all need to learn.

When we cannot avoid a bad thought, we can swap it.

One example involves sleep.

Sometimes haunting 'failure' words can keep us awake.

Repeating a word like 'sleep' can override a bad word.

Our body listens to the word that wins this struggle.

"What you feed your mind, will lead your life." — Kemi Sogunle

Anxiety comes in many forms.

All forms are painful.

The best forms are painful *and* productive.

Fear, worry, and self-rejection are not productive.

Talking in front of a class can be painful *and* productive.

Skill and confidence grow in such moments.

Thus, we find productive anxiety is necessary to life.

Painful anxiety finds us limping along in distress.

Productive anxiety finds us stretching for our potentials.

"To venture causes anxiety, but not to venture is to lose one's self. And to venture in the highest is precisely to be conscious of one's self."
– Søren Kierkegaard

It is helpful to understand everything has a learning curve.

That means there is a start, middle, and end to learning.

We all start out as amateurs. Then we learn how to get better.

With practice, we can get good, but never perfect.

This means that not knowing how to do something is okay.

What is not okay is not recognizing the need to learn stuff.

We should ignore our critics, but never our call to learn.

"The more that you read, the more things you will know. The more that you learn, the more places you'll go." — Dr. Seuss

Everyone is graced with special gifts.

Including the most impaired, diminished, and uninspired.

Sometimes those gifts are apparent; sometimes they are not.

It does not matter.

What matters is that we step over our limits and build.

That takes courage, because the world mocks independence.

Ironically, it gloats over and celebrates inadequacy.

Nature relentlessly shows us how to grow and overcome.

An acorn becomes a tree by first falling down.

"Without ambition one starts nothing. Without work one finishes nothing. The prize will not be sent to you. You have to win it."
— Ralph Waldo Emerson

Rejecting the carpentry of our parents and others takes work.

Rebuilding what they have broken takes even more.

We cannot help what we start with.

We can only determine what we end with.

It is our decision, and ours alone.

We can get stuck with a life we were given and do not like.

Or we can decide what we do like and work toward it.

We get to decide – and then we have to make it happen.

"The greater a child's terror, and the earlier it is experienced, the harder it becomes to develop a strong and healthy sense of self."
— Nathaniel Branden

Unhappiness is a team sport.

The path to personal despair usually unfolds like this:

1. Our head, heart, hand, and spirit are in a good place.

2. Something hurts us, and it takes our heart to a bad place.

3. Our heart then kidnaps our head into bad thinking.

4. Our heart and head then recruit bad behavior.

5. Eventually, our lonely spirit is also corrupted.

We cannot help that our heart will get hurt.

We can learn to resist letting hurt kidnap the rest of us.

If we can do that, the team will pull our heart back.

"People say things meant to rip you in half, but you hold the power to not turn their words into a knife and cut yourself." — Rupi Kaur

Imagine a tug-of-war where the strongest side wins.

We cannot control what the world around us does.

Nor can we control what family, bosses, or friends do.

We can only control what we do.

Depression and anxiety often indicate an effort to control.

The more we do that, the more we lose control of us.

We try to control the outside and thus neglect inside.

Life is about learning to manage our inside.

God has the rest of it.

"Be not angry that you cannot make others as you wish them to be, since you cannot make yourself as you wish to be."
— Thomas à Kempis, The Imitation of Christ

In a cloudy world, the good stuff is often hidden.

Our true nature and that of life can get lost in the fog.

We can easily find ourselves stumbling, darkly bewildered.

In such times, we need to rely on our moral compass.

Sort of like a pilot does when they fly through a cloud.

Everything may look dark and gloomy in the moment.

The sun will soon reveal itself as it melts those clouds.

"The world is indeed full of peril, and in it there are many dark places; but still there is much that is fair, and though in all lands love is now mingled with grief, it grows perhaps the greater." —J.R.R. Tolkien

In a hard world, it is doubly important to grow every day.

That growth need not be in giant leaps.

Ants move mounds of dirt one grain at a time.

But our head, heart, body, and spirit *all* require our care.

The one we neglect will be the one that undoes us.

It sounds like a lot of work, and it is.

In a hard world, we mostly just get to choose our hard.

"Life's under no obligation to give us what we expect."
— Margaret Mitchell

In a crazy time, it helps to have a sense of humor.

The will to giggle, smile, and wink at absurdities cushions us.

Life is too irrational to treat too seriously.

Responsibly? Yes. Seriously? No.

The more seriously we treat the bad, the more power it has.

We may need to address it, but we need not absorb it.

Soft spots sparkle when we laugh.

> *The real reason that we can't have the Ten Commandments in a courthouse: You cannot post "Thou shalt not steal," "Thou shalt not commit adultery," and "Thou shalt not lie" in a building full of lawyers, judges, and politicians. It creates a hostile work environment.*
> – George Carlin

Mom-Dad families are proven as the **best** place to raise kids.

That is not the only place – but it is definitely the best place.

In every kind of family, everyone has a job:

• **Children** – *grow, grow, grow.*

• **Teens** – *keep climbing across that icy melting bridge.*

• **Parents** – *protect, love, support, teach, stimulate, and model.*

• **Grandparents** – *a twinkling eye of acceptance, combined with measured doses of wisdom, seasoned with a pinch of spoiling.*

The family is the bedrock of any healthy society. Societies that discard their families lose their way.

We thus do well to work extra hard to preserve good families.

We are not doing that.

The homemaker has the ultimate career. All other careers exist for one purpose only – and that is to support the ultimate career."
— C.S. Lewis

Raising kids?

Our two most powerful tools are our *love* and *example*.

Beyond that, our job is to insure five things—

1. *Structure* as a foundation for growth.
2. *Successes* that help build confidence.
3. *Safety* – both physically and emotionally.
4. *Skills* training to prepare them for the real world.
5. *Spiritual* opportunities that secure good values.

Simple, yes, but not necessarily easy.

The world is always busy trying to kidnap our children.

Agencies, officialdoms, schools, and others have great power.

But no one can replace parents unless parents let them.

We impair bad influences through relentless engagement.

"The way we talk to our children becomes their inner voice."
— Peggy O'Mara

Is there a genuine sanctuary from the stress of life?

In fact, there are very few truly safe places.

But there is one that truly stands out – being *present*.

The minute we embrace *now*, we leave the past and future.

In fact, this is the only way we really escape internal stress.

Staying in the moment as much as possible is a tranquilizer.

Contrastingly, the past and future are stress stimulants.

Safety of this kind is not a place, but a state of mind.

"Nothing has happened in the past; it happened in the Now. Nothing will ever happen in the future; it will happen in the Now."
— Eckhart Tolle

There are ten natural laws that we cannot dodge.

Try as we might to hide, these ten flavor our universe.
1. Most skills are *perishable*.
2. What we *own* in turn owns part of us.
3. Life quickly decays on either side of *now*.
4. There are a lot more than *seven* deadly sins.
5. Good *choices* are the #1 determinant of hope.
6. *Equality* cannot be given – it must be achieved.
7. Enabling is toxic to all, *love* is a medicine to all.
8. We are not exempt from a *self-correcting* planet.
9. Nothing is free – we dependably get what we *earn*.
10. Joy, peace and gratitude are *renewable* resources.

It is impossible to live well without these nurturing truisms.
We need not be perfect, but we must be dedicated.

"It is an eternal law of our universe that everything shall always return to harmony and equilibrium. Well- being is our default, natural state. Stay strong in times of darkness. The light will soon return. It always does."
— Anthon St. Maarten

Hard experiences, words, and people can recycle within us.

These adverse echoes can easily become a source of hurt.

Clearing our head of old stuff is like taking out the trash.

And it is necessary for the same reason.

One of the signs of old clutter is a brain that never stops.

It can flag old head, heart, hand, or spiritual garbage.

Thinking to learn and let go is a good thing.

Thinking where we are just rearranging old thoughts is not.

Some experiences merit recycling – some need to be tossed.

"Sorrow looks back, Worry looks around, Faith looks up"
— Ralph Waldo Emerson

Chapter Fourteen
Hard or Soft?

There is a difference in hard moments and a hard life.

Most of that difference can be tracked to taking care of those little spots of light and joy that – per deeper understanding – we might now call our '*Softspots.*'

We are born into this world with our fair share, but how the world treats us in our early years can take a toll on our gifts.

God grants children resiliency for a reason. There are no scars from youth that cannot be overcome and turned to blessings. To do that we must recognize, nurture, protect, and properly apply our *softspots* with greater energy than we grant our miseries.

It is important we make sure others do not steal our *Softspots*. It is equally important that we do not steal theirs. It is doubly important that we do not steal our own.

– Which Way Did He Go –

Over time he noticed a pattern.

It was sort of like actor-director Clint Eastwood and his extraordinary western themed movie 'Unforgiven.'

Serving in both roles, Mr. Eastwood courageously attempted to create a film that was entertaining, captivating, and honest – all in the same package.

He succeeded in no small part on that last part by his willingness to portray his characters in the clear light of reality. They were all – without exception – a mixture of good as surely as bad, light as surely as dark, and virtue as surely as evil.

And, so it is with the rest of us. We are all a mixture of positives and negatives that are never firmly anchored in one place.

On reflection, over the course of a life, he recognized that he had never actually known anyone who was truly good or truly evil.

Yes, there were people who were mostly evil, but there were always hidden kernels of softness buried amidst their rubble.

Yes, there were people who were mostly good, but here too, he was always – with time – introduced to points of imperfection.

He determined that good and evil clearly exist and that efforts to pretend that nothing was good or truly evil were actually a form of evil unto itself.

Certainly good can be twisted into evil and evil can be falsely marketed as good. But both clearly exist and we are thus required to be careful detectives in determining which is which as well as the side we elect to work for.

Like the character's in Mr. Eastwood's movie, we, too, will land at a less than perfect place. But we will be able to become, depending on our vision of who we want to be, a 'mostly' of one side or the other.

Through this observation, he landed on another deeper truth.

Who we become rests not in our genetics, our upbringing, our color, our gender, or our fortune or misfortune. Who we become is birthed in our choices.

We have the power, no matter our circumstances, to choose to be a good person or something else. No matter where we are, who we are with, or what life throws at us, we get to choose our goodness or lack of such and no one can take the power away from us.

That, is a glorious place to be...

Ten Hard Truths

1) Happy ever after doesn't exist, but miserable ever after surely does.

2) We rarely get more from life than what we merit, and more times than not, success is dependent on our own efforts.

3) We are born alone and die alone, and the in-between leans in the same direction.

4) Every shortcut to happiness ends at the edge of a cliff.

5) Anger always lies as it hides our flaws and deeper truths.

6) Something for nothing doesn't exist in nature, and anyone promising such is a swindler.

7) What we do, we become.

8) Ample, cheap, and good do not exist in the same space.

9) Happiness is never harvested without effort and contribution.

10) The absence of love explains most personal, material and social problems.

Ten Softer Ones

1) Hope is birthed out of acting, not waiting for luck, magic, or a hero.

2) Every obstacle has hidden exploitable weak spots.

3) Victory and tragedy are not to be trusted – they are both imposters.

4) The more we reach up and out, the taller and bigger we grow.

5) Worry is the toll we pay to drive on a free road.

6) A short-course on life can be found in the heart of a dog, eyes of a cat, and the wings of a butterfly.

7) We are almost always hardier than we or others know.

8) The quality of our life is determined less by what we face than by how we face it.

9) When we give what we need, we get what we need.

10) The seeds you plant in the world will grow most bountifully in your own backyard.

Chapter Fifteen
Softspot Wisdoms

There are certain understandings that stand the tests of time, experience, and reality.

Think of such wisdoms as fertilizer for the good in life, and for the potentials that rest within all of us.

What follows are fifty of the strongest points of insight in The SoftSpot.

Some things are worth repeating.

– You Never Know –

The day COVID hit, I did seventy-five pushups and eighteen chin-ups without stopping, ran for 30 minutes, hung upside down for several more on a gravity bed, worked nine hours, and walked an additional twenty minutes with my dog Pepper to finish the day.

By the next morning, I was unable to hold up my head, and within a week I was in the hospital. I stayed there in one fashion or another for two and a half months – including five weeks on a ventilator.

The part about exercise is not bragging. It is for contrast. I went from being a fit older guy to a wreck in a day. As I recover and write this, I'm still a bit of wreck.

Without my wife, prayer and higher authority's grace, the lingering blessings of exercise, and a parade of wonderful medical caregivers, I wouldn't be here. Actually, per the odds of being that sick for that long, and the dependence on a ventilator, I should not be here.

But here I am. Now I have to put whatever time I have to best use.

I have had to learn to talk, walk, and eat all over again. Having lost sixty pounds – very little of which was fat – up to this point in time I've gained back ten. Due to on-going nausea and gastro distress, most of my meals are a bit forced.

Okay, enough of that.

I am off oxygen. I have a Total Gym on the way to begin the physical recovery process. I can now walk twenty minutes – minus a walker – without stopping and collapsing.

I am beginning to write again – you are reading some of that right now – and it's hard work for a weary brain. But it is also good medicine.

The biggest thing with my writing is working to complete the ten percent left on a book I had almost finished right before I got sick. I am so grateful God gave me more days to put the cap on this long-term effort.

This book is a part of honoring that second chance...

– Wisdoms –

Conflict is a normal part of the human experience. The goal is to make our part of that conflict as mature, productive, and positive as we can muster in the face of the harsh hurdles inborn to conflict.

We begin life pretty much at the mercy of others. Time shifts the accountability for who we are and how we overcome our hurdles to our own hands. Our past explains our struggle, but it does not relieve us of the accountability for pressing on and growing to better places.

Sex as a casual act is made difficult and likely impossible by a human heart emotionally connected to every part of our body.

Intelligence is like gold buried in a mountain. It is of no use until it is dug up and processed into something of value. It takes all of who we are to do that. That is why AI (artificial intelligence) will never replace the power potential of a fully educated and operationalized human being. It will compete – it will not prevail.

Addiction is an over-dedication to anything that crowds out normal living. All addictions are a form of robbing our ourselves. It is not the thing we are addicted to that gets us in the end – it is the gradual drain of our *soft spots* that seals our doom in one fashion or another.

Life provides us with a parade of problems that make it necessary to identify possible solutions, pick one, and continue until we find something that works. Circular stress puts us on a merry-go-round that traps us. Cutting the loop and bending it into a linear stress we can address is a skill that takes practice.

Guilt is designed to get our attention, not punish us for bad behavior. Once it has our attention, it should go away. Holding onto guilt is like carrying a pack full of rocks. A good conscience will find us owning and learning from our errors, and then throwing those rocks down so we can face the additional challenges that are always ahead.

The world is full of predators who take advantage of circumstances that make us vulnerable. We should not allow such people to turn us away from the potentials for good in something that they chose to turn to the bad. A bad person does bad things, but that does not mean all things around them need become equally bad.

Technology is highly addictive and like all addictions it will crowd out that which is normal and good. The big problem with technology is that it is sneaky. It is an easy addiction to hide, and it consumes you one itsy bitsy bit at a time.

Immaturity and mental illness are different like rain and a flood are different. It is helpful to remember that the first helps create the latter.

Love that is in our hands is more dependable than love that is in the hands of others. The suggestion that the best way to feel loved is to give love sums it up perfectly.

People food is like all other foods. It comes in good and bad forms. Too many chips and bowls of ice cream is not good for your health.

Focusing on what we cannot control instead of what we can control is a guarantee of frustration and failure. One cannot be a victim and an equal at the same time.

We are not planted here to exist. We all have our special capacity to touch the world.

Neglecting, ignoring, or destroying our gifts always carries consequences. Opportunity never comes without matching responsibility.

It takes longer to build a person than to destroy a person, much in the same way it takes longer to build a house than blow one up. It is remarkably easy to become a human demolitionist, blowing up yourself or others.

Our world is constantly tempting us toward selfishness or surrender. The road less traveled has us focused on simply trying to do what is right.

People grow regardless of what is done to them. The problem is that excessive hardship means we do not naturally grow in a good direction, and we can wear out sooner than we are designed to.

The good things in life are not free. They must be won, and in the right way.

There are bad things in the world that appear to be good, but are anything but. Figuring out which is which takes experience and effort.

Becoming a good person does not come by accident. We must work for it, and we never get to stop.

What looks tough quite often is not, and what looks soft can be anything but.

Most of the bad things of life wear a false mask of strength and goodness.

Addiction is the ultimate flag for proximity to bad things or bad choices.

Pain is intended to be less about suffering than learning.

We cannot avoid stress; we can learn to control how we respond to it.

We are free to endure, lament, succumb, or learn from misery. These are our only options.

The life of a dedicated victim is seldom a path to happiness or security.

Hard things have the capacity to make us weaker or stronger. That outcome is determined by how we face those hurdles.

We do not come into the world powerless.

Good things are not to be taken for granted lest they be lost.

Some things we lose cannot be replaced, and thus should be guarded with diligence.

Not all things that are important can be seen.

Similarly, not everything that is important is easily defined or understood – or labeled.

Arrogance is almost always a shell that conceals inadequacy, selfishness, fear, and/or ignorance.

We are not defined by what others think of us – we are defined by what we do, what we strive for, and how we measure up to the standards set by our higher power.

Though the world may relentlessly cry "steal from your bucket!", we need not listen. A deeper look at how that theft impacts those who follow such advice serves as ample warning.

Feeling good today at the expense of tomorrow is a relentless temptation. But when one comes to understand how quickly today passes and tomorrow comes, the futility of that approach is revealed.

Any relationship that finds you sacrificing core values, stuck in please and appease, or holds you hostage is not a relationship – it is an arrangement, and it has not been crafted for your benefit.

We cannot help that our body will decay with age and time. We can slow it down, but not stop it. The rest of us – our head, heart, and spirit – remains free to grow, thrive, and reach for the stars. Three out of four is pretty good.

There is nothing wrong with trying to make people feel better. But if making them feel better becomes a substitute for their personal responsibility to be better, we are enabling – and that is a poisonous relationship to all involved.

In children and adolescents, identity development is a fluid process. Our sense of self does not really begin to jell until we become adults. Even then, it is a life-long journey. Great care is necessary during this vulnerable period of life.

Anyone who refuses to debate, entertain the existence of legitimate opposing views, or enter into open discussion is in grave danger of becoming a convert to dogma at the price of wisdom, growth, and maturity.

Truth remains the scarcest, most expensive, and illusive commodity in America's current culture. That misstep in character and commitment is perilous whether at the personal, family, community, or national level.

One way to judge the wisdom of others is to see how well their approach works for them. People who are only happy when they are in control do not offer an example encouraging duplication.

That we can be happy all the time is an illusion found only in Hollywood and the fantasies of creative minds. Note that such narratives are not sustainable beyond one-hundred and twenty minutes.

A child often learns the danger of a hot stove by testing and touching that hot stove. Most of us will touch thousands of hot stoves over the course of our lifetime. The most important thing is not those erred touches, but whether we learn from them.

Unforgiven and stored mistakes can quickly turn our brain into the equivalent of a garage full of junk. We can lose our ability to park our car out of the elements and park good and useful information in our head.

Excessive worry is the mental equivalent of leaving your car's lights on overnight. It accomplishes no good end, but it will drain your battery and leave you stranded.

We cannot control the world, but we can absolutely pick and choose what part of it we intentionally participate in. Finding ways to walk around, away from, though, over, or under the world's absurdities is not easy. But most of the time, there is a way to find a path of escape to sanity.

Whatever we are doing we are getting better at. It thus remains exceedingly important we be doing good things more often than the not-so-good.

Chapter Sixteen
In the End

There are certain truths of life that travel with you as dependable companions. The best of these quietly nudge you toward that which is good, fair, and just.

You will never know all the reasons for your life journey or the impact you may have along the way.

What you should know is that you do not get to stop trying until you draw that last breath.

You should also know that if you work to travel well, there is softness to be found on the path and at your final destination.

There are some truths that are exceptional at helping you be exceptional.

Living is not meant to be easy – it is challenging by design. Amidst your trials you will find friction – that when played with grace and perseverance – births growth, character, and strength...

That which is soft is not always feeble, and that which is hard is not always robust. It takes independence, deeper thinking, and grit to discover which is which...

Karma – the concept that you get from life what you put into life – controls the switch that controls your future...

If you did not live in a world filled with both good and evil, you would not have the remarkable power of choice. With it, your life is blessed with relentless and extraordinary opportunities for exhaustion or exultation...

For the same reason one benefits from an invisible ingested nutrient in a bite of food, the crucial value of the search for spiritual clarity cannot be prudently ignored...

The words love and responsibility are universally linked to the potentials of a life of progress and impact. Anyone attempting to sell the merit of one without the balancing influence of the other is lost in that universe…

You are faced with a daily challenge – the pursuit of comfort or growth. The choice you make most often will more surely be the one that flavors your destiny...

In a fallen world, the only reliable point of fairness is the power you hold to determine how best you respond to what that unfair world throws your way...

It is through words like balance, responsibility, liberation, creativity, skill, maturity, and prudence that you can craft a life of meaning and joy. It is foolish to believe any of us can find a way to good places via bad means...

It is not what you do not have that defines your life course. It is what you do have, and how willing you are to squeeze the juice out of every single drop of it, that makes that determination...

You will most surely succeed in taking care of your *softspots* by helping others in taking care of theirs...

In Closing

Keeping our life journey fresh boils down to two things –

(1) take care of your softspots and (2) know it is never too late to reverse course if you have missed that mark.

Just knowing that you have unseen resources that require you to nurture them for them to nurture you automatically puts you on a safer and hopeful life course.

This book offers insights, tools, and skills. In your own good hands rests the responsibility of practice.

For those with the curiosity, commitment, and character to work toward a more positive life of exploring, learning, and acting, there is much to be gained.

Some of those benefits are of the moment. Think peace, confidence, health, maturity, influence, growth, and opportunity. In each and every case, these outcomes stand as testimony to the care and feeding of your gifts.

But there is a bonus. For those with the will to press forward, there is hope for a special landing – *The SoftSpot* – a time, place, and state of being where all your parts come together in unforeseen fashion.

But even that is not the end. A life spent employing your *softspots* to good purpose is not over when you leave this world. It can be well argued that your best is yet to come...

Nature Boy - Nat King Cole

There was a boy

A very strange enchanted boy

They say he wandered very far
Very far
Over land and sea

A little shy and sad of eye
But very wise was he

And then one day
A magic day he passed my way

And while we spoke of many things
Fools and kings

This he said to me:

"The greatest thing you'll ever learn
is just to love and be loved in return"

www.ingramcontent.com/pod-product-compliance
Lightning Source LLC
Chambersburg PA
CBHW011521070526
44585CB00022B/2494